THE CATHOLIC

By the same author

Fiction
THE GHOST OF HENRY JAMES
SLIDES
RELATIVES
THE DARKNESS OF THE BODY
FIGURES IN BRIGHT AIR
THE FRANCOEUR FAMILY
THE FAMILY
THE COUNTRY
THE WOODS
THE FOREIGNER

Non-Fiction
DIFFICULT WOMEN

THE
CATHOLIC

DAVID PLANTE

CHATTO & WINDUS
LONDON

Published in 1985 by
Chatto & Windus · The Hogarth Press
40 William IV Street
London WC2N 4DF

British Library Cataloguing in Publication Data

Plante, David
   The Catholic.
   I. Title
   813'.54[F]   PS3566.L257

   ISBN 0–7011–3969–2

Typeset at The Spartan Press Ltd.,
Lymington, Hants
Printed in Great Britain by
Redwood Burn Ltd,
Trowbridge, Wiltshire

PREFACE

———— • ————

A young nun told us one morning during catechism class how missionaries from France had been captured and tortured by the Indians in America. The Indians stripped the missionaries naked, tied them to stakes, then pressed red hot tomahawks to their flesh. This was done to them because they were Catholic and loved God. The nun's face, in her fluted wimpel, was flushed. My knees were shaking.

When I left, imagining I was following a narrow path through the dark woods to my home, I felt I was in danger of being stopped by Indians, who would wrap a blanket around me and bundle me off to a clearing where they would undress me.

My family was part Indian from my father's side. Though he and some of my brothers had straight, black hair, black eyes, strong cheekbones, large noses, I did not look at all Indian, but had my mother's blue eyes. If I were captured, I would say, "I am an Indian, too," but they wouldn't believe I was one of them.

I was seven years old and had attained, according to the Church, the age of reason, so was about to make my First Communion, which was the subject of my catechism lessons. The Indians had appeared unexpectedly, as they had a way of appearing, during the last lesson.

At the supper table, I asked my father if he knew any Indian words.

"No."

My mother said, "I know a story about Indians."

"Does it have Indian words in it?" I asked.

My mother, who shared French ancestry with my father, had translated, for the son of Irish neighbors – he was studying French in college and not doing well in it – a small part of Chateaubriand's *Atala*, a class assignment, and kept a copy of the translation. She read it to me. My father listened, too.

This was the story, told by Chactas to René, a young Frenchman in America, in the year 1725.

Many years before, Chactas, a Natchez, fell in love with Atala, a Muscogules. Their tribes were at war. Chactas, when captured, was saved from torture and death by Atala, the daughter of the chief, Simaghan. Atala was Christian, and wore a gold crucifix on her breast. Chactas and Atala escaped into the Allegheny Mountains, where, in a dark forest, they had to stop because of a storm. Chactas protected Atala from the thunder and lightning and wind, and Atala told Chactas her story. Suddenly, they heard a dog barking.

I became, at this point, wary of what was to appear from the forest.

"An old missionary, carrying a lantern, came upon us."

He struck me as strange, this missionary with a lantern in the forest.

"Atala was at his feet in an instant, telling him she was Christian."

I thought: She must have spoken the missionary's language.

The missionary, who might, I had a feeling, have done something bad to them, took the young Indians to his grotto. He said he would instruct Chactas in the Catholic faith. The missionary and Chactas made up a soft bed for Atala to repose on and the men went off to the Mission, where Chactas would get his instruction.

"We started out and soon we arrived and stopped at the foot of a large cross. It was here that the missionary celebrated the mysteries of his religion."

I vividly recall an odd sense from this: the mysteries of my religion celebrated in an Indian forest.

When Chactas and the missionary, named Father Aubry, returned to the grotto, they found Atala ill, and about to die.

"Atala's voice grew weaker and her suffering was intense. She seemed to be waiting for something and, when I told her I would embrace the Christian religion, she uttered, 'It is time to call God here.' I fell on my knees at the foot of the bed, and saw Father Aubry open the chalice and take between his two fingers the host, white as snow, that he placed on Atala's tongue. Then he took some cotton, dipped it in some holy oil and rubbed her temples. 'Father,' I cried, 'will that medicine give her life?' 'Yes, my son,' he replied, 'eternal life.' Atala had expired."

The rest of the translation I heard with a kind of awe.

"That night, we transported her precious remains to the opening of the grotto. Father Aubry rolled her in a piece of linen, woven by his mother. Atala was resting on a bed of mimosa and in her hair was a flower from the magnolia tree. The missionary prayed all night. I sat in silence at her head. The next day, I carried Atala, and with Father Aubry preceding us we marched to her final resting place. We dug her grave and when it was finished I placed her there and picked up a handful of earth and, taking one last look at my beloved, I sprinkled some over her face until her features disappeared."

I felt everything give way in me.

"Upon leaving, I fell on my knees at her grave and cried, 'Sleep in peace, in the strange land.' That is my story, René, and many years later I, feeling very old, am looking forward to a reunion in Heaven with my Atala."

The evening before my *première communion*, in the bathtub with my younger brother, both of us jumped up and down in the shallow water as if it were a stream and splashed one another. No one came into the bathroom to tell us to stop. Our thin, hairless bodies fell against one another. When we drew back we stood looking at one another. My brother and I concentrated, with bright halos of attention, on one anothers' prepubescent members, and I said, suddenly, "Ainque les Peaux Rouges ont cela." ("Only Red Skins have this.") My little brother didn't deny it. We were different from anyone else.

1

———•———

I often thought, in my teens, that I would like to distance myself so far from myself that I would see the dark, angular-faced, blue-eyed person I was as someone apart from me, and I would try to account for someone altogether different. Though I would use the first person, I would be thinking always in terms of the third person, so "I" would think "he" and he would have nothing to do with me.

I believed that a person shouldn't think about himself. I thought about myself all the time. Other people thought about themselves a lot, and did so with pleasure. I imagined this was because of what they had to think about in themselves. What I was helplessly drawn to thinking about in myself gave me great displeasure. If only I were able to consider myself as someone different from myself, he would maybe give me something else to think about.

This someone became my college room-mate.

Sitting at my desk in our room, I heard shouting from the shower room, and I went in. Charlie was in one of a line of occupied cubicles, the plastic curtains drawn back, and he and other dorm-mates showering were shouting and laughing. I associated this image of Charlie, not in retrospect but at the moment it occurred, with everything that was outside me. Though we were both male, I imagined I was so different from Charlie that we didn't share a sex. I had often seen Charlie naked, sometimes with a vague sense of disgust at his white skin and pink nipples, but when I saw him now it was as if he appeared

I

before me for the first time. His body gleamed from the hot water, which flattened his crew cut, ran in rivulets down his face, neck, shoulders, arms, chest, thighs, groin, and sprayed off his cock; a fine line of hair ran, like a dark rivulet, from his navel to his streaming pubic hair. I knew Charlie, but, suddenly, I didn't know him.

His popularity – and he was very popular, elected President of the Freshman Class – was, I later imagined when I saw him on the campus talking to a group, the popularity of his body, which was not covered but suggested by his shirt, chinos, buckskin shoes. This body shocked me, but I did not know what it meant. It was as if I became aware that, unlike some time in the indefinite past, I was now living among people who had taken over where I'd lived, had chopped down the woods and built houses and criss-crossing roads. They took it for granted that everyone had the same kind of body as they. I must take my place among them, must, in a way, become converted to their ways. Charlie's active body was that of someone from the outside world.

I tried to disassociate Charlie's body from him to make it a body in itself. I liked it that he was irresponsible, and quickly became unpopular as the Class President because he never appeared at meetings. This should have made his body, too, irresponsible, but, despite Charlie, it retained its vast associations; relevant to a world I didn't know, it was free in that world to do everything. I loved Charlie and admired him for being Class President, but I was a little pleased when he was impeached and someone else took his place.

We had conversations from our beds in our dark room.

I told him I was making a very great effort not to think about myself, but it was difficult.

Why shouldn't I think about myself? he asked.

It was wrong, I said.

Wrong?

Well, I said, I didn't like it.

He asked me if I'd read Walt Whitman, who thought about himself all the time, but who obviously liked it.

I said I couldn't read Whitman, he was on the Vatican's Index

2

of Forbidden Books.

"The Vatican?" Charlie asked. "You let yourself be determined by the Vatican?"

"I do, yes."

"That's quaint," he said. "You're a quaint person, Dan."

"I resent it," I said. "Of course I resent being told what to do."

I thought he either fell asleep or didn't want to hear about my resentments.

In a bookshop below the campus, I decided – in the way one decides to do what one knows one shouldn't and therefore taking full culpability – to buy the poems of Whitman. I went with the book back up to the campus, and in the front row of seats in the auditorium in the library where I often went during breaks between classes to study or sleep, I opened it. I read:

Oh my body!

This startled me.

> I dare not desert the likes of you in other men and women
>   nor the likes of the parts of you,
> I believe the likes of you are to stand or fall with the likes of
>   the soul, (and that they are the soul,)
> I believe the likes of you shall stand or fall with my poems,
>   and that they are my poems,
> Man's, woman's, child's, youth's, wife's, husband's,
>   mother's, father's, young man's, young woman's
>   poems,
> Head, neck, hair, ears, drop and tympan of ears,
> Eyes, eye fringes, iris of the eye, eyebrows, and the waking
>   and sleeping of the lids,
> Mouth, tongue, lips, teeth, roof of the mouth, jaws, and the
>   jaw-hinges,
> Nose, nostrils of the nose, and the partition,
> Cheeks, temples, forehead, chin, throat, back of the neck,
>   neck-slue,
> Strong shoulders, manly beard, scapula, hind-shoulders,

3

and the ample side-round of the chest,
Upper arm, armpit, elbow socket, lower arm, arm-sinews,
  arm-bones,
Wrist and wrist-joints, hand, palm, knuckles, thumb,
  forefinger, finger-joints, finger-nails,
Broad breast-front, curling hair of the breast, breast-bone,
  breast side,
Ribs, belly, backbone, joints of the backbone,
Hips, hip-sockets, hip-strength, inward and outward
  round, man-balls, man-root,
Strong set of thighs, well carrying the trunk above,
Leg fibres, knee, knee-pan, upper leg, under-leg,
Ankles, instep, foot-ball, toes, toe-joints, the heel –

The body, which was Charlie's body, took over my entire attention. His body was a country with its own special gravity, where I believed I would get everything I wanted. I was not sure what I wanted, but the moment I got to that other country I knew that what I wanted would both be revealed and realized.

To go into that country and live there and have everything, I made love to Charlie. During an early spring break he and I went alone to the lake home where I used to spend summers with my family. The house was cold from being shut up all winter. I forcibly imposed my body on Charlie's.

In the morning, I woke to find he had gone. I searched the cold room. Dead insects lay on the wooden floors. I dressed and went out to find him. The trees were dry and brown, and through the bare branches I could see the lake, on which the ice was breaking up. I walked now in one direction, now in another. For a while I stared at a leafless bush covered with red berries. The woods were silent. Then I went along the rutted dirt road out of the woods, thinking he might have decided to walk to the nearest town on the other side of the lake, get a bus into the city and a train to Boston. When I saw him coming along the road, I stopped and waited for him. He smiled.

"Hi," I said.

"I went out for a walk," he said, and smiled more.

4

We never mentioned the night before.

The transformation in me, I imagined, was total. Of course it wasn't, but I felt it was.

To be free of myself was to be free of my religion. But that I couldn't, according to the Vatican, love Charlie's body and love Christ's at the same time was not really the reason for my sacrificing my love of Christ. What made me decide that I loved Charlie and didn't love Christ was that Christ made me think about my sinful self, whereas Charlie removed me from my world to one where there was no thinking about yourself and therefore there were no sins.

On a Sunday morning in my parents' house, awake and waiting for my father to come into my bedroom and tell me to get up and get ready for Mass, it occurred to me that God did not exist. I lay in my bed, filled with joy. I was a little late for Mass.

The image of Charlie's body relieved me from all my past thoughts and feelings. My soul came alive in me, and I honestly imagined I was starting a new life. What was promised was that my new life would be made by going away, which was to go into the world around me, inhabited by people whose relations with one another were free.

2

————————•————————

Walt Whitman's poetry never appeared in the house I grew up in. The fine trembling that had spread over me as I'd read him for the first time wasn't only sexual, but was the wonder at how Whitman had given me the sense, from so many particulars, of his whole body, amazing in its wholeness. It was as if he had looked in a mirror and described what he saw. I could never see my body whole. I saw only ears, navel, toes, etc.

My wonder at this wonder came from a course in epistemology I was obliged to take at the Jesuit college I attended.

I tried to understand how Whitman had managed to give me a pleasurable sense of the whole body. My excitement in his pleasure expanded into a sense of everything, everything all together, and from this sense rose the idea that I could, in a body, have everything, all together. This could occur to me, not in mine, but in the body of another. And I wanted to know how it did occur.

The image of a man's body, but not a woman's, was to me the image of everything.

Whitman had written about his love of women: "Fast anchor'd eternal O Love! O woman I love!" But he wrote differently about his love of man: "I ascend, I float in the regions of your love O man!"

Of course, I knew I could not have everything. Everything easily broke down into particulars, too many to take in. There was no way of experiencing directly that wholeness. Yet, I wanted to experience it. I wanted everything.

Making love with my room-mate, whom I loved, promised it but did not give it to me. Afterwards we went separately to our homes. When I saw him again in our room at college, less than a week later, he said, "We should cut classes this afternoon and meet at the Fine Arts Museum."

I liked it that Charlie was irresponsible towards the outside world, but I did not like it when he was irresponsible towards me. I waited for two hours on the steps of the museum. It was bright out, and once or twice I thought I saw him come up the steps in the brightness.

Inside the museum, I wandered from room to room. I stopped when I came to the Attic statue of a boy's torso. From time to time I looked beyond the small, headless, armless, legless, sexless body and out the large windows to the spring trees. Each time I looked back at the statue it appeared to me, on its supporting rod, to hold itself more tensely still, and I thought how strange it was that I should feel in the torso an intentional stillness. I looked round to make sure I was alone in the room; I got near the statue and delicately touched a finger to its thigh, then quickly withdrew it.

I wanted the inaccessible body.

It came to me that that torso, in the warm spring light, was more naked than any body I had ever seen. Because it was stone and I couldn't really attribute to it the nakedness of skin I raised my hand towards it with the temptation of what was deeper than skin. I wondered where the sense of its completeness resided in it – in the same way Descartes wondered where the soul resided in the body, and decided: the pineal gland – because the statue was so shattered. Again I put out a hand, not simply to touch, but to push the statue over; above the fragments its nakedness would hover in the light. Someone came into the room and I stood back.

Just as it was impossible to see everything together, it was impossible, I thought, to see the body. You never saw the body. You saw toes, etc. Yet you were aware, as an apprehension, of the whole body. How?

In my scholastic philosophy, our instructions in dogmatic

logic led us above logic, for the irony of such dogma was that, remaining in itself strictly logical, it should attempt to prove what could not be proven by logic. It gave us every reason for rising above logic to apprehend the idea of God in faith, which came, in a flash of grace, from God. Logical thinking was, in the end, made infinitely vague, because infinitely inaccessible to reason, by its ultimate purpose, the existence of God.

I was, I thought, being vastly ironical. I did not believe in God.

I thought impressionistically because I was not good at reasoning. Was an idea what preceded an argument, or was it the conclusion to an argument? I didn't know. But I did know that to have an idea was not, in itself, to reason. An idea was, in a way, like an image, the image of the body and the idea of everything being similar in that they *occurred*. An idea was a bright sense of something being centered. The great mystery was why the vague bright idea should occur.

The idea could only occur in the same way God occurred, with grace. Without that grace, I would not even be able to see a body.

I went around to the back of the statue. Its buttocks were chipped, and there was a scar-crack diagonally across its back. I saw it against the light from the window, and it appeared black.

Outside the museum, small blossoms from the trees streamed through the air. I walked down Huntington Avenue to Symphony Hall, then slowly down Massachusetts Avenue, and more slowly down Commonwealth Avenue. The whole body beyond the shattered body could exist everywhere, at a street corner, in a passing car, in a window, and you looked for it. And sometimes you saw it. In someone you stood by at a corner waiting to cross the street, you saw the image of the body glorified and immortalized by grace.

The windows of the brownstone houses were open, and students were sitting on the sills or leaning out to talk to others on the sidewalk, and others were lounging on the stone steps. Sometimes they touched one another on the elbow, the shoulder, the cheek.

3

———— • ————

Outside a fraternity house, the door and all the windows open wide, a girl, wearing a sweat shirt and shorts, was talking to some men. She leaned in towards them, a hand out, and as I passed her, the men, five of them, closed round her.

At the end of the avenue, I stopped and looked across into the Boston Public Garden, where the light was green.

Entering the Garden, I pulled off my sweater; with my sweater I pulled out my shirt tails, and, as I was tucking them in, I thought, No, and I let them hang out. Inside the Garden, I unbuttoned my shirt and felt the air against my chest.

Off a curve of the path was a bank of grass, and I stopped on it. I practiced, in my mind, sitting in the least awkward way, as if I thought everyone was watching me to see how I would do it. I was not sure how I did it. The others on the bank of grass, which swelled up behind me and sank away into a hollow, were lying flat, and no one looked at me. I, too, lay flat. The grass was humid. When I sat up quickly, I was dizzy.

A group of three young women were sitting on a bank of grass on the other side of the path. One had her back to me. Her back was bare, and tanned, and when she leaned more towards the others the curved edge of the red dress came away and revealed the white skin of her body. The other two girls were listening to her talk. I saw her hands move. Her arms dropped and she turned her head away from the others, so I saw her in profile, frowning a little, as if she were thinking. One of the other girls was now talking, moving her hands. Perhaps the one in the red dress was thinking about what she said, or what she was hearing, or both. Then the third girl spoke.

They seemed to be in big business, and were discussing that, and the business was complex and required a lot of talk. I felt that if any one of them had been left waiting by someone for hours, she wouldn't assume it was her fault and accept it in that way, but would think out, even discuss with others, why that person hadn't shown up, and decide if she'd ever see him again. What these young women were seriously discussing was the rights of a person who made a date and broke it. I believed that person had the right to do whatever he wanted, but they didn't, and I wished I could hear, in the same way I wanted to hear how a big business was run, what they said about him.

The girl with the red dress turned towards the others and spoke, her hands raised. One of the other two, facing me, started to plait her long hair loosely at the side of her neck, listening all the while. When she saw me looking at her, she flicked her loose plait over a shoulder and said something to her friends, so they all turned quickly towards me, then as quickly to one another, and they closed in.

After a while, I rolled over and lay looking at the sky. Then I sat up.

The girl who had braided her hair was combing it out with her fingers. She drew the strands out and up to the top of her head with one hand and held it piled on top with the other. She pulled up the long strands at her nape. When she placed both hands on her hair it hung in thick loops under her fingers. She smiled at me, lifted her hands, and her hair fell.

She scratched the side of her nose and rose a little, and for a moment I thought that she was going to come over to me. But she shifted her weight and looked away from me and continued to scratch her nose.

When she lounged back to listen to the girl in the red dress, the third girl, in a white dress, shifted to the side to give her room.

Though I couldn't see her mouth move, I saw the hands of the girl in the red dress move, more and more, as though she were stating her final decision.

The girl in the white dress unstrapped her sandals and took them off and pressed her toes into the grass. Her neck was smooth, her chin rounded, and her nose was round and smooth. The straps of her sleeveless dress were tied at her shoulders, and the thin white cloth hung away from her body.

I studied the details: her lower lip, the small, inward curve of her jaw into her earlobe, the shine high on her cheek, her temple, the downward curve of an eyebrow.

She appeared to be outside the talk of her friends, thinking of something that had nothing to do with them. Then, wincing, she looked up at the girl in the red dress and spoke briefly, after which they were all silent.

The other girl sat up and drew her fingers through her hair.

While the girl in the red dress talked again, the one in the white slowly ran the tips of her fingers along the top of her bodice, inserted her hand under, and held a breast.

As if the meeting had been called by the girl in the red dress, she ended it. She was tall, and her black hair was pinned up on her head. She talked down to the other two, who looked up at her.

I heard her say, "Well, then to hell – "

The two got up and, the girl in the white dress carrying her sandals, they all left.

I sat for a while, and got up and walked.

I rambled deeper into the Garden, towards the pond and the bridge, and on the bridge I stopped at the rail. Below me, one duck swam, its wake gurgling. I leaned my elbows on the stone rail to study the duck, which beat its wings against the water and flew off.

I crossed the bridge, then went down stone steps to the edge of the pond, and I crouched at the water's edge. The layers of light and water appeared to separate, and a fine layer of water, I thought, floated over a deep layer of light. From behind me someone threw something into the pond, and, startling me, the water and the light rose up in one bright spurt.

As I walked along a path I saw, alone in the middle of a green bench, the girl in the white dress. Some people passed between us, but once they passed she and I looked at one another.

This had to be thought out. It was like asking a girl at a hop if she wanted to dance. I always wished that the girls had to ask the boys to dance. Within three steps, however slow, I didn't have much time to think. People going past me walked in a speeded up way. I thought I had to talk to her because she expected me to. At least, I had to turn round to her and make a gesture – hunch my shoulders and raise my hands – to let her know that I'd like to stop but I had to go on and there was nothing I could do about it, and that way I wouldn't hurt her. I felt, suddenly, free to do anything I wanted. She wasn't looking at me. Standing in the middle of the path, I pushed my shirt tails under my belt, and as I was buttoning my shirt she did look at me. I went quickly to the empty bench across from her and sat.

Go on, I said to myself; do it.

I got up from the bench and stepped onto the path, out in front of a pedestrian who bumped into me. The girl on the bench laughed. I let the pedestrian pass, then I went straight to the girl and sat, without looking at her, at the end of the bench.

She leaned back and said, "You did that pretty well."

"Not very well."

She smiled. "Pretty well."

Though I didn't know what her business was, I knew it determined people's lives, and she couldn't have been over five years older than I. I was nineteen.

"Maybe we could take a walk," I said.

I let her lead the way, back towards the pond, over the bridge, and through the Garden to the gates on Charles Street. We were silent. I could not imagine what she was thinking. Across Charles Street, we sauntered onto the Common, our bodies, side by side, sometimes bumping at our hips.

At the side of the cement footpath was a black man on a bench, bent far over and placing cards, face down, on the cracked cement. In front of him another black man was standing looking now down at the cards, now along the path. The man setting out the cards was saying, "Choose a card, any card." The standing man, just as we were passing, pointed to the top of the seated man's head and said, "That one." The man with the cards turned one over and announced in a loud voice, "You got it, you won ten dollars," and held up a bill. The girl stopped, and when she did the seated man lowered the hand with the ten dollar bill.

She asked him, "How do you play this game?"

The winner, who hadn't been given his ten dollars, folded his arms.

She said to him, "I know you're the con man."

The seated black man gave her a demonstration. They were all laughing.

When she looked round to see where I was, I went to her.

She asked the men, "Do you guys know of some place where we can play pinball?"

"Not any place you can get in," the dealer said.

"You don't know me," she said.

He laughed. The other man didn't laugh, but winced.

She said to me, "Come on. We'll go find a place."

She set the slow pace. We crossed Beacon Street, and I followed her up Bowdoin Street.

"Maybe we'll find some joint around here," she said.

She turned left, up the street behind the State House. Policemen were at the back entrance to the State House.

"In there, maybe," I said.

"For sure."

I was playing, and I wanted to, but I felt that I was playing against a sense of desertion, as of something general having gone out of the world, leaving only details, and all that could be done with the details was to play with them.

She told me her name was Jessica.

Mine, I said, was Dan.

I studied her blond hair swinging against her bare shoulders, her arms, the clavicle above her white, ruffled bodice.

Her silence made me think I must talk, must show her that I was interested in her. When I asked her about herself – "Are you from Boston?" – she talked about all the building being done in Boston. I wondered if she was trying to impress me with what she knew.

We turned into Louisberg Square.

13

I said, "There won't be a pinball arcade here."

She squinted at the windows. Then she asked me, "So what would you like to do?"

"Anything."

I led her down Beacon Hill, and on the way we sometimes separated to get round the garbage cans on the sidewalk. At the bottom, on Cambridge Street, we paused to look, beyond fences made of long sheets of plywood, at a vast building site. Around stark cement towers bulldozers were digging. There was water in the holes, and there were heaps of black earth by the holes. I asked her what was being built, and she told me. Maybe, I thought, she was working for the city. She was interested. She put everything together, as if all the millions of atoms of which the building scheme was composed were held together by her in the shape of a chair, or a shoe, or a milk bottle. She did this easily.

She kept talking as we went along Cambridge Street, past narrow restaurants with dirty windows, shops which sold automobile parts, and bars where, I thought, we would find pinball machines.

She was leading me. We turned to our left, back up Beacon Hill, along the brick sidewalk. Towards the top of Joy Street she stopped at a wooden house, painted lead grey, its steps worn down to the wood.

"This is where I live," she said.

I thought she was waiting for me to say I'd like to see her place.

When she went up the steps, I followed her. Through the small panes of the wide living room window was a magnolia tree in blossom. The room was warm. I thought she was crossing the room to open the window. A step from me, she seemed to have forgotten where she was going. She placed a hand on the side of my neck, then she went to the window, unlocked it and opened it.

I asked, "What do you talk about when you're with your girl friends?"

"Why do you want to know?"

"Because I wondered."

"Men," she said.

She raised a foot and slipped off one sandal, then the other, and threw them under the wing chair, which she sat on. Her dress rucked under her.

I sat in the middle of the velvet-upholstered sofa, silent. After a minute, I stretched out on the cushions, my head resting on one bulging arm, my shoes hanging over the other. I turned my head to the side and smiled at her, slouched in the wing chair. She drew her fingers through her hair. She looked me over, from head to shoes, one corner of her mouth lifted.

If I were in her arms, everything would be all right. But so much had to be thought out before that could happen. To make love with her would be to enter into some kind of business with her, and the agreement required careful attention. To put my arms around her, to kiss her, to insert my hand into her bodice might take all the consideration of committing my life to her. It would take a very long time for me to say, "I love you." She didn't move when I got up from the sofa.

After I dressed and kissed her and said good bye, I asked, "Can I see you again?"

She answered, "No, you can't."

I drew back. She was smiling.

"I think we'll make this a once upon a time deal," she said.

I left relieved that she didn't want to see me again.

4

—————— • ——————

I remained close to Charlie after we graduated from college and both of us, for a short time, lived in Boston. We met often to have lunch or supper in delis, or to go to bars.

He liked to show me the drawings he was doing at life class at the Boston Museum of Fine Arts. These were of large, nude women, done in conté crayon with thick, black strokes. They impressed me. I would have liked one of the drawings, as much for the big women who stood naked before Charlie, as for the drawing. He didn't offer one to me, however.

Then he showed me a series of drawings of a young woman, slender and yet full at the same time, both dressed and undressed. Charlie gave me one of these drawings. Nude, the model was lying on a bed.

I recognized her from the drawings as soon as I saw her. She was at a table with Charlie in the small upstairs restaurant where he'd asked me to meet him for supper. Charlie was pleased to introduce me to Roberta.

I could understand a man making love with a woman, but I could not understand a woman making love with a man. A man could easily hurt a woman by making love with her, even if it was only to chafe the skin of her face with his beard. I thought that women must find men, if not dangerous, painful. Charlie's blond beard was stubbled about his chin, and at the table I noticed Roberta look at it, look at his ears, eyes, nose, as he talked. I could not grasp her attraction to him. Surely, Charlie was, to her, too big, too rough. Surely, she didn't want to make love with him. And yet she did, I saw, because of what was most unfeminine about him: the hair curling over the neck of his undershirt, his veiny hands.

All the while Charlie talked, he gestured. He pressed the tips of the fingers of one hand together as if holding out an atom, too small for anyone to see, yet elemental; and his talk revolved and revolved around that atom, or I imagined it revolved around it because, as I couldn't see the atom, I didn't really see the point of Charlie's talk. He opened his fingers and raised his hand higher and higher, and, as he did, his voice also rose, to make his appeal heard by the world. I was embarrassed for him. I thought Roberta would suspect him of being a phony. I wanted to pull him away to be alone with him so I could listen to him talk without the worry that others would think his talk was nonsense. It was filled with his sense, as expansive as his smell. (Living with him I'd become familiar with his smell.) But Roberta enjoyed him.

His open palm held over his head, he was saying, "Now, my idea is – "

His body gave his talk subtlety, or whatever subtlety there was in it. That was Charlie's secret: he was able to infuse his words with the beauty of his body, and while you listened to him you sensed the warmth of his skin in words which would otherwise have been dead. Was it because of this that Roberta indulged him, I thought. But my sense of Charlie was mine, not hers; hers had to be different. For me, if it hadn't been for his body, Charlie would have been a fake, would have been as embarrassing to me when we were alone as when we were among people who frowned after the first five minutes of his talk. By the way she laughed sometimes, with a hard edge, I imagined Roberta might easily be seeing Charlie was a fake.

She and I ate and Charlie, gesturing with his fork, talked, and I wondered what I would do if she suddenly decided she didn't like him. I felt that it was my responsibility that she should. She must have liked him or she wouldn't have been with him, but I had the feeling she could, at any moment, change her mind, and I didn't want her to change her mind. If she decided she didn't like him, she wouldn't like me either.

17

Laughing, she said, "You're so funny, Charlie."

Though she didn't say much herself, she could, I knew, have taken over the conversation and talked Charlie into silence with a sentence. But she kept him talking by asking him questions, laughing. Her narrow, ironical questions sent Charlie off into wider, unironical airs. Or maybe he was more ironical than I thought. She must have been making fun of him, I thought, by asking him the questions she did, and he, smiling at her before he took them up, must have seen that she was; but he seemed to respond to her irony as if it were affection. I always treated Charlie seriously; maybe he didn't want to be treated seriously. She seemed to see ironies in Charlie I hadn't ever seen, not until now.

She was wearing a sweater, and a gold chain round her neck, and her heavy blond hair appeared almost wet when it swung as she leaned forward. The V at her neck showed soft skin; the fine chain was stuck to the side of her neck. I imagined that her covered arms, the sleeves pushed a little way up her wrists, and her covered breasts were bare.

I was unsure about the differences between sexes, and could only distinguish them by the feelings they aroused in me; and I noted, as I'd noted in the presence of many women, that Roberta's body was, to me, fixed solidly in her personality, which, being a unique personality, made her body unique, so it was as if she, as each woman, had her own sex. There was not a female sex.

To me, all men belonged to the same sex, and men did not have fixed personalities, nor fixed bodies.

Worried by the way Roberta would react to Charlie, because her reactions, being that of a woman, were unpredictable to me, I watched her more than I did him. To understand her meant studying the details of her body, all of which were, I thought, details of her self. As I felt I already knew her well enough to see that her personality was in her control, I felt that her body was in her control, and she could make it do whatever she wanted it to: she could decide she was sexually attracted to, say, dwarves. I imagined she was capable of peculiar sexual attractions. I never thought men's sexual attractions could be peculiar, because they did not depend, as they did in Roberta's case, on a choice, but on not being able to help their attractions, which were always larger than themselves. Roberta determined her attractions, and if she decided she wanted to make love with a dwarf, she did, and if she decided she didn't, she didn't. But there was no way of knowing – no way of my knowing – what made her make her decisions, and what might make her, suddenly, change her mind. She liked Charlie now. I wanted her to like him, and not only because in liking him she would like me; I wanted to because, in liking him, she became a little more general than she was, and I was not so worried by her.

All at once, she placed her fork on her plate and she sat away from her chair-back with her hands in her lap and her shoulders slumped. Her lids were half lowered as she looked at Charlie in a way she hadn't before, and he stopped talking.

Charlie brought some food to his lips, chewed a little, and, his mouth full, started to talk again, and to smile. He talked to no one but her. If I'd been talking, I would have tried to say what I thought she wanted to hear, though I'd always be unsure what that was. He talked as if he knew what he was doing. He knew she was listening to him.

I saw her lean slowly backwards till her shoulders rested on the chair-back. When she said, "You really are funny," her voice was low.

And here I remarked another difference between men and, from my point of view, a woman: that men were "visionaries", and she, Roberta, was – Charlie laughed, loud – "political." I almost wished Roberta wouldn't indulge Charlie, but reprimand him for being stupid. I should have reacted by saying, Charlie, you really can be stupid. But Roberta didn't, and I didn't.

A glow rose to his face, and with the glow a wide, wide smile, and he himself became, for a moment, an inhabitant of his bright world.

Blood rose to the surface of my skin, and I felt my penis turn.

Roberta reached across the table and touched Charlie's cheek. He was startled and laughed. She laughed.

Afterwards, Roberta told Charlie she wanted to walk with me alone and talk a little. Charlie put his hands on our shoulders he left us on the sidewalk to go in the opposite direction. I thought that Roberta would talk about Charlie, but she didn't. As she talked about Boston, we walked more and more slowly, and sometimes we stopped in the middle of the sidewalk.

Roberta's body drew me close to her for the warm smell that came off her.

Outside the house where she lived, I held her for a moment before saying good night. She might have thought I did it to let her know I was, in my way, happy about her relationship with Charlie. I was happy because with her I felt that the world was without ghosts, that objects – stones and trees and water – were not haunted by presences, that people were not lost souls.

5

——————•——————

After I left Boston, I lived in different cities, some abroad, for five years, and then I returned to Boston. At twenty-four, I was beginning to know a little what I felt towards men and women.

To me, men were like the inhabitants of a city, all character-ized, as New Yorkers or Londoners or Parisians or Romans were, by their city.

A woman was incomprehensible to me for her individuality, and I was more interested in her as a person than in any one man; I was not interested in men as individuals, but I wanted to live in their city.

I had a job teaching foreign students English in a private school.

On Friday and Saturday evenings, I went to a bar (near the bus station) where only men went. During a holiday week in the early summer, I went to the bar often, when the sun was still high. After the glare, I could not see the walls or floor or ceiling, but red bulbs fixed at crazy distances from one another in the darkness. The hot bar smelled of cigarette smoke, beer, damp cement, and sudden whiffs of cologne. As soon as I had bought my bottle of beer and stood at the bar, swigging, I looked at the barman.

His long arms bare to the shoulders, reaching in all directions as though at once, he opened bottles, poured out drinks, placed them on the wet bar. His sweaty neck and face gleamed in the red light. A kind of official, he knew the laws of the place, because here there were no written laws but laws by precedent. He was young, but he knew everything. Listening to someone describe a broken affair, he smiled and wiped his hands on a towel. Watching him, I drank down the bottle of beer and then ordered another. Whenever I asked for a beer from him, I felt that I was serving him.

The bottle held out, I turned to face the room. In turning, I exposed myself, as if I became naked. I held the bottle of beer up higher. I caught myself making many small adjustments to my body; leaning on the bar and bending one knee then unbending it, putting one foot before the other then moving it back, drawing in my stomach to let my belt sling further down my hips. I tried to make myself stand still.

Among the red lights, three men, not far from me, stood leaning together, talking. Whereas everyone else seemed to walk about as if not quite sure where they were going, these three stood at a center, turned away from the rest. They didn't notice me. I raised my bottle to my eyes to see how much beer was left in it. I didn't belong to any country, really, so they could not make me feel, if it ever occurred to them to want to, that I was excluded.

Thrusting myself away from the bar, I swung my bottle up, drank, and walked about the room swinging my bottle. I wanted everyone to think I was there by some momentary choice, and as soon as my beer was finished I would leave.

I was, myself, my own country, different from and above any other.

At the back of the room, in a corner, was a wide metal door with an illuminated EXIT sign above. The sheet metal was dented, and around the edges were cracks of light from the summer evening outside. If I pressed the bar, the door would open, and I would find myself in an alley.

Nothing should come of the possibilities aroused by people of the same sex being drawn together, and yet some promise, as elliptical as a body smell, held me. All together, but not singly, these men possessed a sex which was different from my own.

Turning away from the door, I drew back when the three young men passed me to go to stand by a pinball machine in a corner of the bar. They wore white dress-shirts, the collars unbuttoned, the sleeves folded back on their forearms. One gave his bottle to another and rolled his sleeves further up his arms, and the other two watched him; he took his bottle again and drank, and the other two continued to watch him. He talked and the others listened.

I studied them all as if from a great distance. A shock came over me when I saw the one with the rolled-up sleeves look towards me, then at me, and I felt that distance contract, and they were all suddenly near. I stood away from the wall as he and I looked at one another. When he turned to the others, I thought it was because he'd been asked a question. As he turned back to me, I stepped forward, not quite sure of my footing, and he, seeing me come forward, turned altogether away from me. I saw his hair, his ears, his nape, the stiff collar, the neat seams of his shirt, his belt, the back pockets of his chinos, the creases, the heels of his loafers.

One of the others was standing sideways to this first one. He was taller, his cheekbones and jaw sharp. He had a more intelligent body, if there was such a thing, than the first, whose body was, after all, dumb. I wondered if the first one said something about me, because the thin one glanced towards me. Our eyes met and I thought: him. But he glanced away.

The third one wasn't that attractive, and yet I looked at him with my expectation aroused, and the more I did, the more I saw he was, really, the most attractive of the three. He didn't look round at me, but the fact that he didn't made me sure that he knew I was there and that he wanted to look. He laughed too much, running a hand through his hair, when one of his friends said something.

For a moment, I felt I was making a choice from among hundreds, maybe thousands of possibilities, and I was completely free. In the next moment, however, that free choice would stop being a choice, and become a need. I would suddenly become possessed by this young man, if I dared myself to think: him. I didn't want him, didn't want what one man had.

He pushed his sleeves up his arms, and they fell back; he undid

23

and did up the buttons of his shirt. His clothes appeared a little damp at the shoulders, arms, curves of his chest, his buttocks, his thighs. His clothes would have taken in the warm moisture of his skin, its smell, and, perhaps, its sensitivity, because the clothes themselves seemed alive. Whereas the clothes of the others stiffly encased them, his shirt and trousers moved with him.

I wanted him. He must have known that I did, because he reacted. When he looked round at me, it was not to reassure himself that I was there looking at him, but to let me know he had his body and I didn't have any, and he almost smiled. He looked away and did smile. In its awareness of itself his body became the most beautiful I had ever seen in my life. He stretched out an arm as if reaching for something, then ran a hand up and down it so the sleeve was raised high. He reached behind a shoulder to scratch, I imagined, the itching cloth at the shoulder and yanked it so his shirt was pulled a little from his trousers. Again he turned towards me and, as he did, he undid the top button and slid his hand inside to touch his chest, and he did it to tell me: this is mine.

By my lowered look I told him: no, it's mine.

I felt our views of one another were controlled by movements of our heads, so that when I pulled, he looked away, and when I looked away, too, just at the moment he looked again at me, he pulled me back. Our faces were impassive. I was almost able to pull him towards me, in little jerks. He said something to his friends. The tall one said something, and they all laughed. They all turned away and leaned in towards one another.

Though I kept my eyes on him for a while longer, he didn't look back.

I walked away and stood in another spot, against a wall.

I caught my body making odd movements.

Then I saw a young man standing along the wall to my right, who, raising his bottle to his lips, lowered it without drinking when he saw I had my eyes on him. He thrust his jaw forward and stuck out his lower lip. First I studied the empty bottle, then the ceiling, then the floor, and then I turned to look towards my left. Someone down the wall on my left was looking at me. I was amused to be between the two, and I glanced back at the first, who was leaning sideways against the wall to stare at me, and again at the second, who was standing away from the wall to face me squarely. Given there was no difference I could make out between them, I asked myself what should make me choose one instead of the other. With only a slight sense of daring, because I didn't care much, I stepped towards the first, holding my empty bottle out to him, but before I spoke he pushed himself away from the wall and left. Quickly, I went to the bar, bought another beer and returned to the wall to stand closer to the second but, as I was taking a gulp of beer, he left.

I thought I should go, and I swigged down my beer to empty the bottle. The door opened and I noticed it was dark outside. The red neon sign on the front of the bar room reflected in cars parked by the kerb. I was sweating.

The toilet was behind the bar. The door was open, and a black man was standing at the bowl. The stream of his pee splashed so much, I imagined it would splash over the edge. I wanted to see him pee, and got a little closer. I imagined that here he wouldn't mind, but he kicked the door shut with the heel of a shoe to finish. I didn't look at him when he came out.

I left the door open when I used the toilet.

When I came out I saw at the bar, alone, the young man I had wanted. His presence startled me, because he had ceased to exist and all I'd retained of him was a recollection. I stopped at the end of the bar, imagining the room was empty except for him. I stepped to the bar and put my hand on it, and, as I did so, he looked up at me, then looked down. It occurred to me: maybe he had been following me around after freeing himself of the others. The bartender came to me and I politely ordered another bottle of beer. He smiled when he gave me the dripping bottle. As I drank, I looked down the bottle at the young man and saw he was looking at me. I lowered my bottle and returned his look as if from a height. I was taking a great risk. He might decide I was playing a game with him, which was worse than my simply not being interested. With his elbows on the edge of the bar and his shoulders hunched so his head lolled, he glanced to right and left, but he kept looking back at me.

I recognized what happened to me when I became possessed. I could hardly take in that young man, except in details: not an ear, but the lobe of an ear; not his neck and chin, but the curve of his jaw under the earlobe; not his hair, but a fine curl behind his ear. And even these details gave way to greater details, details of points of light against darkness. I knew what was happening. It had happened before. Of course, I knew the horrors, but the horrors came later, and what came now was that sense, that deepeningly amazed sense, of something happening for which you will give up everything. This happened to me only with men, and only with men I didn't know. Among them, I didn't have to do anything, didn't even have to move, and it happened.

My pulse pumping, I kept telling myself: You must do something.

But I didn't want to do anything. I thought: It'll happen, and you'll have him.

No, I thought, it won't happen unless you go to him.

He pushed himself up from the bar, walked along it and came round the corner. He stood in front of me, his face stern.

A total self-possession came over me.

He had a low, resonant voice. His name was Henry. He was Bostonian.

None of this mattered. What mattered was his body, so near me I could have reached out and touched it. From the exposed parts – his hands, his wrists, his forearms, his neck, the glimpse of his clavicle under his open collar – I tried to imagine all of it.

I wanted to be modest and say things that would interest him, not about myself – because I didn't think that would interest him – but about Boston.

When he leaned towards me to hear better in the roar, I thought I sensed the warmth of his moist body. I leaned very close to his flushed ear to speak.

For a locked moment, we leaned towards one another.

He drew away and said something and I answered, eagerly, "I know just what you mean. I'm like that, too."

His brow lowered as if I had said something, if not wrong, at

26

least out of place, and he wasn't going to answer me. He said, "Excuse me," and he walked away, across the room to someone, and they talked.

I tipped the bottle up to drink more, but there was no more in it. Rolling the bottle between my palms, I stared at the bartender.

What I'd done wrong was to talk about myself.

The bartender came over when I raised my hand. I asked him for another beer.

When I looked across the bar room again, the two were gone.

I wandered around with my beer.

You shouldn't be able to bear yourself for the embarrassment you cause yourself, I thought.

I knew these moments, too. They were more familiar to me than any other kinds of moments, and they could turn me, if I didn't turn against them, into someone I would despise: someone who tried to live in the strict terms of his false self. I had met many who did. Perhaps I didn't have enough style to assume a fine edged cynicism which allowed me extravagances of emotion and reasoning. With that cynicism, you could do anything and you remained irreproachable, to yourself even more than to anyone else. You would never embarrass yourself. It might have been that I had not embarrassed myself enough, as I was sure some men I'd met had, when they'd been as young as I: embarrassed themselves so deeply, so often that all that could save them was cynicism in a grand style. In some, much older men, the style had terrified me, not only for its cynicism but for its grandness. I understood these men. I had met some, and respected some, but, really, I could not be one because of my sense of risk. They could not take what to me was the greatest risk: the risk of embarrassing myself by pretentions so vast I was a fool to risk them.

Someone tapped me on the shoulder.

6

———— • ————

The warm, clear night was high and wide. Walking beside him, I didn't ask him where we were going.

He talked about Boston.

We entered the Public Garden. The darkness there expanded under the dark trees.

He too had, I thought, the sense that we were going anywhere, to do anything. And we knew that whatever we did, it needed no consideration.

We climbed Beacon Hill, then down the other side, where he lived in a narrow, brick building.

As he opened the door to his apartment, I wished, suddenly, I were back in the bar. I didn't want one person, didn't want someone who lived in a particular apartment in a particular building on a particular street. I followed Henry into the small entrance hall, where he turned on an overhead light which made his hair shine.

Without thinking I grabbed his head and he tried to draw it away. I yanked it back, closer, to kiss his eyes, nose, his mouth. He held my hair, turning my head at angles to kiss it all, to wet it with his saliva. He pulled my shirt out of my trousers as I pulled his out, and, still pressing together and kissing, our noses and chins knocking into one another, we wedged our hands between our chests to undo one another's buttons and pull our shirts off. As I pressed, writhing a little, against his exposed chest, more revealing of him than anything else I could know about him, I felt rise in me the sudden impulse to say, I love you.

I licked his cheek, his ear. He dug his fingers into my back to press me closer to him, so close I felt that if he let go we would spring away from one another, and, keeping me so tensely close, he sucked at the side of my neck. Again I wanted to say, I love you.

When we drew away from one another it was only long enough to kick off our shoes and pull off our socks before we drew in together again, with a force that had us pressing as though to hold each other, kiss one another, more deeply than our arms and lips could. I forced my tongue into his mouth, his nostrils, his ears, and his eyes; his face was slippery with my saliva. While I kissed him, he drew his thighs away, undid my belt, unzipped my fly, and shoved my underpants down with my trousers. My erection got caught in my underpants, and I released it with a finger; then I slid off my trousers and underpants and, as he looked down and watched me, I unbuckled and unzipped him and pushed his trousers and underpants down to his feet and he stepped out of them. We remained separate, looking at one another. It seemed to me I had expected him to have another sex, one different from mine, different from any I'd known. He looked up at me and smiled.

As he stepped towards me, I stepped away, out of the light, so he wouldn't see my body.

I had not made love often. The first contact with another's body was still, to me, the most amazing sense the world allowed.

Our arms around one another, we went into his living room. We didn't get as far as his bedroom. As if he couldn't go further, he pulled me down onto the sofa, where, on the cushions, we thrashed and bounced, locking together and unlocking our arms and legs. One of the cushions slid from beneath us, another flipped up. From a point of view above us, which I took from time to time, we were fighting, not trying to break one another down into one position, but trying to break one another into many positions. Over him, on my knees, his legs between mine, I clenched him in my arms and lifted while he tried, his arms clenched about me, to pull me down. With a wrenching motion, he turned us over and our bodies fell apart, but we hung on to one

29

another, he about my neck, I about his shoulders, and he twisted a leg around one of mine. I tried to turn him over, and we dropped off the edge of the sofa. I fell on him, and he immediately locked both his legs around mine and held my arms so I couldn't move, all the while kissing me. When I tried to kiss him, he drew his head back; I strained my neck forward to reach him with my mouth, but couldn't, so rocked up and down to try to kiss him, and when I did he bit my lips. On the floor, we rolled over and over, and each time we did, as with a spasm, we unlocked our arms and legs and locked them again in another position. Sometimes, my face pressed into the side of his neck, or his shoulder, or a buttock, we strained our holds on one another so our muscles and tendons stood out and we remained motionless, until, again spasmodically, one of us let go, and we rolled into another position. We were sweating and our bodies slid against one another. I licked his armpit, his navel, and sucked at his erection. I felt his body convulse as he shouted, and that convulsion and that shout made me shout, too. We remained on the floor, holding one another. When he fell away, our sperm drew out between our stomachs. He lay back loosely on the floor, his arms extended over his head, his eyes closed, and I lay sideways by him.

He rolled his head towards me and asked me, hoarsely, if I would spend the night.

"If you want me to," I said.

"I want you to."

I felt everything in me give way to him.

His body was wet and his hair was thick with sweat. He raised himself heavily, as I did, then I followed him down a passage way into the bedroom, where the bed was unmade. Dun light came in from down the passage way. Tangled in the top sheet was a towel; he pulled it out, wiped his stomach, and gave the towel to me. It was stiff with dry sperm and it scratched. I threw it on the floor and lay down on the bed beside him. He lay on his back, his arms folded under his head. The wrinkled sheets smelled of body odor. The room was hot. As if it occurred to him all at once that I was beside him, he turned his eyes to me; he looked at me for a moment, his face stark, then raised himself and leaned over to kiss me. His eyes closed, he fell onto his back again, his arms by his sides, his legs stretched out and separated, his cock lying backwards on his pubic patch.

Propped on an elbow, I scanned his body, and my sense of it was of there being too much of it to see, to touch. And while trying to take it in, fixing on the details – the little fold of flesh at the arm pit – you knew you were missing what gave the real shape. You never saw what counted, but what distracted you. You thought the exposed details didn't count, but something else did, which was not invisible, but visible if only you could see it. Finally, you knew that the details seemed to distract because you saw them as parts, not all together, and it was only in seeing them all together that you'd know what drew you with the concentration of someone possessed. But there were too many details to take in, to take in and remember. Presented with an infinity of cells, how could you bring them together so that the cells disappeared and a body appeared?

The apparition of the body was your own doing, and you had to strain your attention to make it appear from such a mass.

He might have been asleep, his breathing light, and I didn't want to wake him, but wanted to touch him. Instead, I pulled at the sheet.

I wondered how many people he had made love with on this sheet. It was penetrated with the presences of how many lovers, their sweat and saliva and whatever sperm hadn't been wiped away by the towel? I smoothed out the wrinkles between our bodies and was reminded of the sheets I used to see in the college dormitory pulled from the beds by women every Monday morning and thrown into piles in the corridors. As I passed them I used to imagine they retained the impressions of all the bodies that had slept in them, had jerked off and maybe made love with others in them, and I wanted to fall into one of the piles. I recalled going down a flight of stairs and turning to see a bundle of sheets tumbling towards me, thrown down by a cleaning woman at the top, and I stood and let the bundle, unloosening, tangle about my legs, then I reached down and bundled it together in my arms and

31

dropped it on the landing. Out of his sheets rose the bodies Henry had made love with. They engorged my possessiveness of him.

He had a watch on, and I wondered why I hadn't noticed it before. The watch seemed to cover him, so he was not exposed as I wanted him to be. It attached him to a country of constraints, and his body, for me to make love with it, had to be a country of total freedom, where we had the right to make love with everyone. I had to take that watch off his wrist. On my knees, I leaned close, slipping my fingers under the band to undo it as carefully as I could. When I got it off, I rose and found Henry staring at me. I placed the watch on the bedside table then, still kneeling, turned back to him. He was now completely naked, the completeness like something beyond one's understanding.

He kept his eyes on mine. He was frowning, and I wondered what he was thinking. When I glanced down to his groin, I saw he had an erection lying back on his stomach. It seemed to me that this could have nothing to do with me. Perhaps I didn't want it to have anything to do with me. I wanted it to have to do with all the lovers rising from the sheets. I looked into his eyes again, filled with thought. He could not, however, have been thinking about me.

What kept us apart was the desire, closely considered, of all the possible ways of making love, and the desire, when we were in each other's arms, to hold all those possibilities open. There was something deeply thoughtful in the way we moved towards each other, he rising as I lowered myself. I was thrown off balance as much by my thinking as by the awkward way I shifted my position. Carefully considering what we were doing, we inserted fingers in one another's mouths, into one another's anuses.

We sat cross-legged before one another, our knees pressing; we ran our hands over each other's heads, shoulders, abdomens, and sometimes one of us leaned in close as the other got to his knees to take the wet head of his cock into his mouth, saliva bubbling and drooling about his lips.

I put my hand on his chest and thought that what I most wanted from him was that he should be different from me, but that he wasn't, he was like me.

For him to be not one man, but many, a countless number, was to promise that one of these many men was different at least in having done what I hadn't yet done. But that meant doing what was beyond arms and legs, cocks and mouths and assholes to do. No multiplicity of men, however great, was any more capable of doing more than one man could do to realize the truly unimaginable. An orgy of men was reduced, finally, to what was familiar. A multiplicity of men suggested involvement with something shared among them, and the more men, the more shared the involvement among them, the more abstract that something was, and the more abstract, the higher above my imagination it went, towards something so different it was not even humanly conceivable. To keep myself aroused by him, I would have to see him as not one of many, but many, too many for love making.

Maybe it was a hairy mole, to the side of a nipple, that reduced Henry's body to a low fact and made it no different from mine.

And, after all, no man's body was really different from mine. All my strained attempts to see the relationship of two bodies of the same sex, not as an image of one body contemplating itself, but of two bodies contemplating one another for the differences that made each appear to the other to be more than a body, were attempts to give spirit to a body that had no spirit. And that was what I did, had always done: started with the spirit and tried to give it body, started with the vague idea and tried to make it a fact, always more interested in the spirit and the idea, because to me they appeared to promise everything. Everything was in the spirit of another's body, and not my own. My own body was without spirit. But so, now, was his.

I knew that no amount of passionate exploration would lead me to discover that he had, in the essential way I wanted, a sex as yet unknown to me.

It wasn't that I wanted him to be a woman.

I wanted him, in his body, to be altogether similar to me and altogether different. The potency of the difference should be great in inverse proportion to the similarity. The more like mine his body was, the more different I needed to believe it was.

I didn't want him to be a woman because a woman's body could not be abstracted from her.

My longing for him to be spirit, and utterly sensual as spirit, was so great it couldn't be reduced to detail. The details of his body couldn't account for what his body did to me in rousing such a longing for something more than those touchable details. He, slouching and loose-limbed, closed his eyes as if he were meditating, and I raised my hand again and placed it on the side of his neck. He hefted his shoulder and lowered his jaw against my hand and smiled a little. The body I was really attracted to, the body I wanted to be aware of at its fullest, was larger than any false idea I might have of it, and it was this that must take me over. Perhaps the difference between us was that he had a spirit in my longing for him to have a spirit, and I had no longing for one in myself.

My hand caught between his shoulder and jaw, he fell backwards, so I fell forward onto him, and we continued to explore one another's bodies.

I wanted to do to him something I had never done before with anyone else. Because my sexual encounters hadn't been frequent, after each one I'd thought it out carefully, not so much to go over what I had done as to figure out what, next time, I'd do that I hadn't yet done. I'd tell myself: remember to run your tongue along the gums under the lips, to run a finger along that puckered ridge between the asshole and the scrotum. In meditative pauses, tracing his outlines with a finger, I wondered what I could do for the first time.

My tongue exuding spit, I licked him, as he lay still, from a big toe, up to a knee, up the inside of his leg, up under a hanging ball, around the pubic patch, at an angle up the groove in his groin to his hip, from his hip to his navel, up the softly undulating space between his abdominal and pectoral muscles to the hollow at the base of his throat, up under the stubble-rough chin and to his lips, which were open. I didn't kiss him, but collected more saliva and spat into his mouth, and he moved his tongue in the saliva before he swallowed. And then I kissed him.

34

At the same time I felt a small disgust, I felt the need to say, I love you.

Whatever we were doing to one another, we were in control, a delicate control sustained by the desire to experiment.

He rolled me over to do something I, even without knowing what it was, would have to submit to. I lay on my stomach, head to foot on the bed, the sheet rucked up under me. I felt his tongue slithering between my buttocks. I felt disgust and love together. I knew what the Biblical "a stirring in the bowels" meant, and writhed as his wet tongue went in. My bowels loose, I could, just then, have shit in his face. I thought: How could anything that so fills me with disgust fill me, too, with a love almost unbearable? And what more disgusting things might make me feel even more unbearable love, so unbearable the only expression equal to it, the only expression that could make it bearable, would be to shit on him?

Then something happened between us. It came over us to go as far as we dared, even if our experiments might go too far and destroy the very freedom which inspired them.

I lay so limply, he rolled me over with difficulty; I lay intentionally passive, arms and legs akimbo. He was kneeling over me.

What he'd done a moment before expressed, for the very intimacy the disgust inwardly suggested, some strangely moving love; now his just touching me on the arm, with an outward suggestiveness of no more than light intimacy, left me cold.

When he grabbed my erect cock in his two hands and jerked it, he said, "Fuck."

I yanked his head down by his hair.

Embarrassment being an awareness of oneself as false, we were attempting to assume, in the falseness, attitudes which would shock. We could have invented entire personalities for ourselves in our expansive falseness, and it was in this, more than anything else, that we could devise acts no one before us had performed.

On his knees, he kept pulling at my erection. He said with a

35

high voice, "Tell me about the people you've fucked with."

"No."

"Tell me."

My voice, too, was high. "Tell me if you've ever asked anyone that."

"No."

"I think you're lying. Are you lying?"

"Yes."

When he said that, I felt a sudden rush up into my erection. "Stop," I said, "I'll come."

"I won't stop."

"I'll come."

"No, you won't. You can control it. Tell me," he said.

My voice went shrill. "I can tell you about the first time I fucked with my room-mate." I laughed. "I don't want to tell."

"Tell me."

I rose up and grabbed his cock and sucked it, my saliva splattering, and when I pulled back I looked at the wet, red, swollen head.

"He had a more beautiful cock than even you have," I said.

He hit me on the cheek with his cock. "No, he didn't."

"He did. Every time I jerk off, I think of it. I'll always think of it. It's a picture I carry around with me that I pray to."

"Are you a fucking Catholic?"

"Yes."

The cold I felt exuded a fine sweat.

"Aren't you ashamed, a Catholic fucking like this?"

"No."

"Tell me about fucking your room-mate."

He hit me again on the face with his cock. I laughed. He hit me again.

"Tell me," he said.

I could make up a pornographic story that had nothing to do with what had happened, like the stories men told one another about the men they'd fucked. As he tapped my cheek, sometimes my lips, with his cock, I said, stopping often to swallow my saliva, "We were spending the weekend at the lake. He said we

36

should play strip poker, so we sat on the floor and played the game. He was the first one naked."

"Did he have a hard-on?"

"No. I said there was a rule to the game, that after a person was naked, if he lost again, he had to be given a hard-on."

"Did he lose again?"

"He didn't lose again until I was naked, then he lost. I sucked his cock. When he had a hard-on, we went on with the game."

"You should be a writer," Henry said. He nudged his cock into my face.

"I said there should be another rule. Whoever lost after being given a hard-on had to be fucked. He said he didn't want to go on, but I said he had to play the game. With his streak of bad luck, Charlie lost again. I grabbed him before he was able to get out of the room and pulled him to the sofa – " I was shivering with the cold sweat, which coated me like thin slime. Henry's cock was sticking up before me, nudging my cheek just under my right eye. I looked up at his face. "I don't want to go on," I said.

He frowned a little.

I laughed. "This is silly."

"Is it?"

"Yes."

The frown went from his face and he sat back on his legs, his hands on his knees. "All right," he said.

As soon as he said this I felt something given up I didn't want to give up but to hold. My blood began to drain out of me. Not sure what I would do, I crawled on all fours up to him, where, on my knees, I reached for one of his nipples and pinched it, then twisted it. He winced a little, looking down at what I was doing, but he didn't say anything. His shiny red erection, sticking up from between his legs, looked ridiculous. I wanted him to think he was a fool for it. My blood rose up again in me when I leaned forward and closed my teeth about his nipple.

We pulled the sheet up from the mattress when he or I grabbed it to hold onto something, apart from one another to steady ourselves, and temptations came over me. They were like inspirations which had no real object; inspired to make love, I

37

couldn't think of anything equal to the inspiration. The temptations were everything, and they surrounded me as if pulling me in different directions to realize them. The moment I went in one direction I would feel myself pulled in another. Not able to act – and, somehow, not wanting to – I nevertheless felt the impulse to act, an impulse that urged, Do it, do it. But I didn't know how to, couldn't, do it. The more we made love, the stronger the temptations became. Sometimes I felt so pulled to one side I thought I must give in, still without knowing what I would be giving in to. When it did verge, suddenly, towards one direction – my chafing the stubble of my beard hard against his jaw for what seemed hours – it would flash in my mind that what we were doing no longer had anything to do with making love. My own body was tingling from being chafed hard. And when he held me, on my stomach with my arms locked behind my back so I couldn't move, as he chafed my nape, it flashed again that we had gone far from sex.

I couldn't believe that he felt what I felt, or, even, that I could arouse feelings in him. If his feelings were in any way like mine at the moment I experienced them, their arousal was caused by what had to do only with him, as if he were at a distance from me and no connections could be made between our feelings. And yet, when he turned me over and straddled my thighs and looked down at me, I recognized in his eyes and the set of his jaw my own sense of wanting to press our love making, or whatever it was we were doing, outside our bodies. It was as if I could hear him thinking, It isn't enough, it isn't enough just driving my cock up his ass, there must be something else.

Whatever he did would be incidental to his need. That need frightened me. He smiled, his wet hair stuck out. As he lowered his face slowly towards mine, I said, with a deep, unfamiliar voice:

"You look crazy."

I stopped him from doing what he was about to do. The moment I saw the uncertainty in his eyes, I grabbed his shoulders and pulled him off balance, so he fell. I clinched my arms tightly about him.

I believed I could do anything. The danger inherent in imagining I could do anything was not in what I would do; the danger was in what I could do.

If I asked myself the question, Could I draw blood? the answer had to be, Yes. Not only was I capable of what was human, I was, too, of what was inhuman. A potent smell emanated from our sweating bodies as I fucked him, he lying submissively, his face crushed sideways into a bare part of the mattress. But fucking him wasn't enough to control everything I was determined to control. I thrust my erection more and more roughly into his asshole. His eyes closed, he grunted. I clenched my teeth, wanting to say something more than "Fuck", some word strong enough to express my desires.

My cock, as I pulled back to thrust in more forcefully, slipped out. I took it in my hand. It was gleaming red, dripping with fluid.

If I used my imagination, really put it to use to invent experiments meant for shocking discoveries, not even the most original imaginings would, finally, appear to me original enough. I was capable of imaginings, I knew I was. I also knew that I would never believe I had come upon the one shocking discovery that all my experimenting was meant for, the one shocking discovery that would reveal all. And because my imagination would keep trying and trying for greater and greater originality, it might try to make of me an original – that is, a grotesque.

Perhaps the great fear was just that of being like anybody else.

But that was backed up always with the fear of what you would do to be extraordinary. The mattress seemed to shift. I knew this sensation of a short, abrupt movement outside me came from the impulse to do the most extreme I was capable of. That wouldn't be a sustained action, but a spontaneous act. I could have – I wouldn't have, but I was positive I could have – cut off his cock, or, more likely, mine, and to do it for no other reason but that it was possible.

Frowning, he raised himself and looked round at me, wondering what I was doing.

39

My erect cock in my hand, I wanted to make a joke. I laughed before knowing what I was going to say. I said, "What a fool's tool."

I saw his frown deepen, and, as I laughed, he lunged at me and threw me backwards onto the mattress. My head hit the headboard, then slid down, so my neck bent and my chin pressed into my chest. My limbs twisted under me, I was unable to move because he pinned me down, and he tried to pin me down more by continuing to lunge at me with his chest, all the while punching my shoulders. My joints, my neck, seemed to lock. All I could do was force myself to laugh in a way to let him know I thought he was just fooling.

He said, "Stop it."

My laughter was false.

He slapped my face. "Stop it."

Perhaps he was just fooling, because I saw him smile, his face so close to mine it blurred. With a wrenching movement, I threw him off me, and was only able to rise before he lunged at me again and pinned me down again, this time sprawled crosswise on the bed. He grabbed one of my arms and was just about to try to turn me over and twist the other arm up my back when I yanked myself free. He tried again to grab one of my arms as I flailed them and, when I unintentionally hit him in the face with a hand, he fell forward onto me so my breath shot out. He slid his arms under my arms, and with one hand dug into a shoulder and with the other held my chin and the lower part of my face and twisted my head to the side. I could have got out of the hold by hunching my slippery shoulders, but I knew he was fighting me, and I remained still. When I tried to turn my head to look at him, his fingernails cut into my cheek; but I was able to roll my eyes towards him enough to see his face, red and running with sweat. His anger couldn't have been caused just by me, nor his desperation. Feelings blew up and separated themselves from us to billow like huge, sweat-wet, windy sheets around us. He snorted. Then he let me go, slid sideways off my body and turned his back to me, his dishevelled head on an extended arm.

His body appeared huge in the still room.

I sat up, breathing heavily. I raised my knees, rested my elbows on them, and looked at Henry.

In a small voice, I asked, "What's wrong?"

He didn't move, and I didn't expect him to. When I felt a stickiness run down my thigh I glanced down to see my drained penis, fluid pouring from it like transparent blood. I was the person to say, Everything is wrong. I looked at his back, his head, his buttocks, his arm, his legs.

I was terrified of everything, as I was terrified of the unknown.

I longed to hold Henry's body.

If I touched him, though, he'd pull away, or push me away.

Frightened, I put a hand on his shoulder, and he immediately dropped onto his back, as though thrown from a height; his head to the side, and his eyes, like his head, rolling a little, he smiled. I leaned over, and, with my unbalanced body falling forward, I clasped him. He, too, had lost his erection. We remained still.

When he kissed me, I felt my body stir in response, and I kissed him. If our kisses were embarrassing to us, we admitted our embarrassment. Not speaking, we were in our speechless embraces and kisses nevertheless close to admitting everything, all the moles, pimples, scars on our bodies.

There was in our love making, somehow, an awareness of the vanity of it, and admitting the vanity was admitting everything. There was nothing beyond the love making, however violent it was.

A great pity for Henry came over me. The pity was entirely for him, and I made love to him as if to commiserate with him for the very fatality of his living skin and muscles and blood. I brushed his hair away from his forehead and kissed it, and then I stroked the sides of his face with both hands.

I did not know if it was my sex which attracted me to death and artifice, but I knew that the easiest fantasy for me, one that occurred of itself, was this: of the pale body at its most beautiful, dead. My imagination, isolated in my skull, engendered images of the body submerged in water, or floating in air, the limbs softly rising and falling in the currents. These images were as easy for me to conjure as metaphors and similes, and I had come to recognize them as products of a mind which tried to make them relevant by believing they suggested more than what they were. The more removed they were, the more I attempted to see in them greater and greater relevance, and that, finally, was the relevance death had. The fact that I should think the relevance could only be made in the image came from the belief that, against death, the image had to survive in itself. I could so easily see the body surviving its death in the holy picture of a dead body, which roused all one's pity.

What made me relevant was what extended me beyond myself. All I could extend myself into, however, was the possibility, as illusive as metaphor and simile, that there was an outside. My overwhelming longing for possibility, in which I looked for salvation, exposed my isolation.

Shifting his weight, he turned me over and lay on me. He held me and kissed my face.

I felt a strange numbness around my erection.

Our love making had to have a meaning, and I would give it meaning.

He tightened his arms around me and held me while he licked my eyes, temples, ears. I turned my face from side to side, not so he wouldn't be able to reach it, but so that he would just be able to reach it, and that slight tension of his reaching out and my drawing back, or my reaching and his drawing back, went throughout our bodies.

I made a crazy act of faith: in the certain knowledge that our love making had no meaning, I nevertheless believed that it did.

Our longings existed as our bodies existed.

All, all of the outside was in Henry's body.

We fell down together as we held one another.

We were two ridiculous young men holding one another.

Our crossed arms rubbed. Henry spit into his hand for lubrication, then kept his little finger out and crooked. It was taking a long time. My wrist was aching. Sometimes, Henry stopped, threw his head back and said, "Ah," and I moved my hand frantically, but nothing more happened, and he started again.

Just when I took my hand from Henry's erection he grabbed my nape and went rigid. I continued. His thighs rose. He shook his head so the sweat switched from it, all the while his chest going in and out with deep inhalations and exhalations. He shut his eyes to wrinkles. I covered the head of his erection with my hand, and I saw the sperm ooze out between my fingers. He fell, the back of his head knocking heavily against my shoulder, and he turned to press his face hard into my shoulder.

I slid my hand, coated with his sperm, up and down my erection as I held onto Henry with my other hand.

I thought, I am a fool, I am a fool, and I ejaculated into the air.

A kind of wail came from me, which surprised me as much as it seemed to surprise Henry. I felt the tension of his hold slowly release, and I, too, released my hold. But we didn't fall asleep.

We lay for a long time, our arms loose about one another, our eyes open but not looking at one another. We shifted a little when he or I felt an arm going to sleep, but we remained awake. His eyelids kept blinking. To pull him towards me and kiss him, as I wanted to do, would have taken energy I found difficult to believe I'd ever had. It seemed a very long time that we lay as we were. At moments, his eyes glanced as if at something outside the bed. When he pulled himself closer to me, I had the feeling he did because he was frightened of what was around us, and when he effortfully lifted his body and lay alongside mine, I felt it was to get away from what he had seen. He lay motionless against me. The movement I felt around us was extended, I imagined, from our breathing, our pulses, whatever moved involuntarily in us under our skins. He was as attentive to it as I was, and we lay against one another waiting for it to rise or fall. Something around us moved like the movements of air about heavily moving, big bodies. It became imperceptible, and then it came back so strongly that, changing all our motions to involuntary motions, it began to move us on one another, to lift and lower our limbs, our heads, to roll us over together. It engaged us in a sixth sense, the most passionate, which controlled us and took us over. At first moving us slowly, heavily, then quickly, lightly, so the impetus made us make wild gestures, and we felt as though we might, at moments, rise from the bed when one of us pulled the other up. Under us, about us, above us, movements struggled with one another, and we had to give in to them. Sometimes Henry seemed to be pressing me down to a level from which I had to force myself up for breath. I had never before found myself making love as though I were being forced to.

We took positions because we seemed to be made to. Henry and I stood up on the bed a little away from one another; his forearm rested on one of my shoulders, the hand of his other arm was on my hip, my arms were by my sides, and our inclined heads touched. We stood like this for a long time. What caused my awe was the recognition that, at this level of love, which should have disallowed all but the most elliptical demonstrations, the demonstrations were at their most affected. We should have been too embarrassed to do anything.

In my religious fervor, I did this: knelt beside him, reached my arms under his shoulders and knees and, hefting him, slid him onto my naked lap, and I held him, loose limbed, as closely as possible. Some low sound rose from my throat.

The greatest possibility in our love making opened up beyond the vanity of our love making, beyond everything we felt, or could feel, towards one another. I couldn't know how it had happened, but we were taken up by large presences about us, so different from us we would, had we been able to see them, have been terrified. They were trying to make us give in. It was only the rank smells of our armpits and groins and our breaths that kept us in our bodies. We were so close to giving in, but didn't, not quite, because we were anticipating the moment when we didn't have a choice. We were thrown at one another, and the impacts of our lunging bodies burned. It was as if we were promised that enough kissing, enough sucking, would turn our bodies inside out, and we would become invisible. The most extravagant temptations shook about us, and our struggle, if it was a struggle, was against the temptation of giving in, which was like the almost irresistible impulse to fall into space.

I was on my back and he was lying on me. I held him about the waist, my face wedged between his legs, sucking at the soft sides of his testicles. Then I drew back a little to look at them swinging between his open legs. His cock was against my chest. On top of me, licking my thighs with sharp licks, he began to shake himself, so his balls knocked against my cheeks and lips. Nothing could make this ridiculous. I felt his warm, wet mouth about my erection as he thrust. I thrust upwards. As I sensed all my senses rush inward and outward, he sucked more and more deeply, so I ejaculated, and he, while I was ejaculating, pulled his mouth away and arched his back and screamed.

We remained loose limbed in that crazy position. When he drew away his sperm fell in a gob on my chest. I rubbed it over my skin.

While we stood on either side of the bed, pulling and tucking the bottom sheet into place and drawing up the top one, our penises contracted. We wiped our thighs with the towel before we got back into bed. Though our bodies were still hot and sweating, we lay in one another's arms.

Henry fell asleep. I couldn't, and lay awake. He kept moving, trying to fit himself against me comfortably. I pulled away, because our bodies, wherever they touched, seemed to melt with heat. Asleep, he moved close again. His face and his neck were wet, and gleamed in the dim light that came from outside the room. He licked his lips and opened and shut his mouth, then he pressed his lips to my shoulder. His breath burned on my skin.

I couldn't sleep for watching him. The dim light smoothed out his skin, his features, and made him pale. It was as if it were only at this moment that his great beauty could be exposed.

I would make blessed objects of his bare shoulder, his arm, his hand, his eyelids, his nose, his mouth.

But I couldn't bear the heat of our bodies. It made him move again, listlessly, licking his lips. As I was at the edge of the bed, there was no margin to move away, and I didn't want to push him away. Sweat trickled over me. I didn't want to lose contact with him, no matter how unbearable, but finally I had to.

Out of bed, I found, down the passage way, the bathroom, where I splashed water onto my face and gulped water from my cupped palms. To cool off, I walked around the small apartment, into the living room, the kitchen, examining the objects of his life.

By the telephone was a pad with names and numbers. They were the names of people of a society which excluded me.

In the entry hall, where our clothes were on the floor, I looked at a framed photograph on a table of a family, a mother and a father and, between them, a boy, Henry, all of them staring out and smiling.

I shut off the overhead light and walked back to the bedroom in the light from a street lamp outside the living room windows.

Henry was lying on what had been my side of the bed, so I went round to the other side and got under the sheet. It was soft, and settled coolly over me. He was asleep on his stomach, his head turned away from me on the pillow.

I still couldn't sleep, and I didn't want him to, both because his sleeping took him away from me and because it opened him to experiences I couldn't share with him. Propped up on my elbow, my head in my hand, I continued to study him, resentful that I had been left behind as he walked through some high, or deep world, which was unfamiliar to me. I had no idea what world his body referred to in any of its social duties. Our love making had nothing to do with daily life, which he reverted to when he stopped making love, leaving me wondering where he'd gone. He'd gone home to his apartment.

Lying flat on my back, I thought I should leave and go to my own apartment. Maybe I would be able to sleep if I were in my bed.

Being in his bed, in his apartment, kept me awake.

And then I began to think of all the embarrassing moments in my life – or I felt that all of them were coming back to me and making me think about them. I thought of the time, in Paris, when I'd said to a young Frenchwoman that I wasn't American, but Canadian. In London, I said to a priest I met in a Catholic church that I was a practicing Catholic, though I hadn't practiced in years. While I was going through a museum in Rome, an American girl started to talk to me, and I gave her a tutorial on

46

early Italian painting, about which I knew no more than what was in the guide book in her hand. Once, in a bar in New York, I told a man I was married and had a daughter. No doubt no one had believed me, and this made it easier for me to support my pretentions now; if I thought they had believed me, the support would be difficult.

The night, like a dream, seemed to go through a cycle.

Yet, I couldn't sleep. I reached across Henry's body for the watch I'd put on the side table and tried to see the dial, holding the face at different angles. I put the watch down.

Instead of lying back, I turned on my side and, again, looked at the body next to me. It appeared so much outside me that it might never have had anything to do with me, not even to have been engaged with my body in sex.

I rose up close by him, then pressed my forehead and my face into his nude back, between his shoulder blades, leaning my weight on him. With a start, he woke, but he didn't move for a time. I drew my head away and he turned over. His face was calm. Half asleep, he reached up and put his hands around my neck and pulled me down to him to fit my head into the space at the side of his neck. All his body felt calm, dry and cool. Perhaps he was more asleep than awake because he went still again and his breathing wheezed a little. My nose and mouth were pressed into his cheek. I began to kiss his face, my lips swollen huge by being chafed, and with each kiss on his growing beard my lips swelled more. I imagined my hands enlarged, too, and my feet, and my entire body. Slowly, as if in his sleep, he began to kiss me in return. I felt his body also become enormous, not solid, but a smooth, thin surface.

His body became very small, as did mine. Our arms and legs minute, we clasped one another on a vast bed, and fell asleep.

I fell into a dream cycle, involving me more in movement than in scenes as it swung me, slowly, downwards, and, going down, sideways, too. Then I began to rise, always, as I did, turning at odd angles. Sometimes I was both rising and falling at the same time.

I woke and didn't know where I was. I sat up, trying to focus

47

my eyes in the almost dark room, not sure how I related to the walls, which appeared distorted, or even to the bed, which also seemed distorted. When I saw a body half covered by a sheet at my side, I didn't know, though I thought I should, who it was. For a second, it came to me that it was my younger brother and that we were in bed together in our bedroom. But this couldn't have been my brother. Lying back, I fell asleep, but woke again and again, never sure in what room, in what bed, or with what person.

Sometimes when I woke I was frightened by what might happen.

Asleep, I dreamed again, and this time, as I was being swung, in a wide curve, downward, someone woke me by touching my shoulder.

I didn't start. In a way, I'd expected to be woken, though I didn't know by whom. It didn't matter that I didn't know who he was. He leaned close to my face and made a gesture which I understood to mean I must be still, mustn't make any noise, because people were standing in the darkness of the room watching us, and we had to escape. He placed a finger on my lips to keep me silent.

Or perhaps he was waking me, not to warn me against those others, but to draw my attention to them as people who wanted something of us, who wanted to take us somewhere and show us something outside. When he clasped my hand, I imagined it was to lead me up from the bed and out, following those others, and there, in the dark outside, he put his arms around me and kissed me.

I didn't understand. Sometimes I was aware of making love with someone, sometimes I wasn't, and yet, all the time, I had the sense of making love, of moving, swung downwards and then, abruptly, upwards, in those great arcs which were the extensions of the motions of love making.

That love which moved us now, so much **greater** than any intentions we might once have had, made us **innocents**, in awe of making love. We had never before made love.

7

———— • ————

In the early morning stillness, I got out of bed, leaving him asleep, and went into the bathroom. In the shower, my nerves felt exposed after the gush washed away the outer layer, like a shrunken skin, of all the bodily fluids, his and mine, which had dried on me. It was as though I were alone in the apartment. Even using his towel, I didn't feel close to him; my feeling was of being at an airport hotel, getting ready for a flight abroad. I picked up my clothes from the floor in the entrance hall and dressed.

I thought I would just leave. If I went back to him he might wake up, and then he might think he had to get up and prepare breakfast for me. I didn't want that. I wanted to go, to start on my trip, to be at the airport early and wander around the terminal. But then I thought I'd have a last look at him.

He lay on his back, the sheet rumpled under him. Sunlight crossed his chest.

As soon as I was outside, I felt I had arrived in a foreign city. It was a good time to be there: Sunday morning. None of the few people I passed in the street knew what a long distance I'd travelled. I had all that sense of possibility you have on arrival. Crossing the Common, then the Public Garden, it struck me as odd that people were doing ordinary things when I felt that everything was extraordinary and that everything I would do in this city would be extraordinary.

In the Public Garden, I sat for a while on a bench in the sunlight.

My apartment was on Marlborough Street, in Back Bay. I ate, then corrected the essays of my students, Panamanian, Israeli, Venezuelan, Belgian, Japanese, Senegalese students who wrote in English. When I finished, it was only ten o'clock. I cleaned my apartment.

About twelve o'clock, still feeling there was so much I could do, and wanted to do, I telephoned Charlie and Roberta. They were married and had a baby son. I telephoned them whenever I felt I wanted to do something and didn't really know what. Roberta answered and invited me for Sunday lunch.

What I felt now was completely separated from what I'd felt during the long night. All my movements seemed light, so light they required no effort. I could have done anything, but this lightness might have come to me. Sitting on the streetcar, I thought suddenly, You're all right, and my happiness seemed to arrive at that moment.

It was as if the person I'd made love with was back in the city I'd left. I realized I hadn't left him my address or telephone number.

On a table spread with a towel, the baby was kicking while Charlie changed its diaper. "Will you hold him?" Charlie asked, "so I can get rid of this?" He unfolded the disposable diaper to show me the shit in it. The baby laughed. Charlie left and I tickled the naked belly of the baby, whose penis flopped up and down as he kicked and laughed. When his father came back and raised his legs to wipe between his buttocks, the baby went stiff, then continued to kick and laugh when his father released him.

In another room, Roberta was talking on the telephone.

"We'll let him go naked for a while," Charlie said. "He likes it."

A blanket was on the floor in a bay formed by three windows, and Charlie put the baby on the blanket and lay on his back by him, so the baby crawled onto his chest. Standing, I watched them play. Charlie pressed his face into his son's stomach, then softly bit the flesh with his lips, then kissed it. I wondered if Charlie was putting on a show for me, was demonstrating to me what privileges a father has with his infant son. When Charlie

50

began to lick his son's belly, so the baby hiccupped with laughter, I was sure Charlie was putting on a show. Whether he had any intention to exclude me or not, the sight of my friend playing with his baby became an icon that had nothing to do with what he intended; this icon existed for me in itself, and I was moved, not by my old friend and his infant, but by a young father and his son. That ability to see someone referring outwardly to the world rather than inwardly to me, I took as a manifestation of my happiness.

Roberta came in and stood by me to watch the show, and after a while she smiled at me to let me know that she saw Charlie was putting it on for me. I always imagined Roberta understood all the complex reasons why a person did something, and I felt she credited me with the same understanding. She assumed that I was more intelligent than I was – more, anyway, than Charlie – and that she and I could communicate as she and Charlie couldn't. We both saw that Charlie was acting, was doing what fathers did before old friends, particularly an old friend who had loved him. Because we understood him more than he did himself, we could indulge him, we could even find him charming. What she perhaps didn't know about me was that, though I had a vivid awareness of the complexities of the human act, I did not have the intelligence to study and sort out those complexities; I was drawn to the image that suggested all the complexities and more. Yet I wanted Roberta to think I was with her, and that my appreciation of what Charlie was doing was, like hers, scientific and large. I very much liked her believing that I was more intelligent than Charlie and saw him more clearly than he saw himself.

"Let's sit down," she said to me, and took me to an old sofa in the middle of the room. She seemed to be saying, We've indulged Charlie enough. When we sat, Charlie stopped playing with the baby and put a clean diaper on him.

Roberta said to me, "I was talking to one of my Indian women."

"About what?"

"They call me up to ask me if I can help when their sons get into trouble with the police."

"Do you?"

"I try. The problem for me is I don't know how far I should go. I tell myself it doesn't matter, as long as I'm studying them."

"Because otherwise it might be painful?"

She laughed. "No. Otherwise it would be boring. My God, it sometimes takes a lot of looking to make a culture interesting."

I wanted to talk about being a Catholic with her, as if she could explain to me, a little, why I gestured and dressed and spoke and ate and shit and made love and slept and dreamt as I did. But she never seemed to want to talk about me. She would talk to me about Charlie, sometimes for hours when we were alone, and she'd question me about his life before she knew him. And she would indulge Charlie when he talked about himself, looking at him closely and listening to him, but never me. I wondered if she did this because she believed I was as interested in Charlie as she was, maybe more interested, and also because she thought that I, who was supposed to be intelligent, would never indulge myself with talk about myself.

She told me a story about the Indians she was studying. She said they had lost nearly all their identity as a tribe, and hardly anyone knew anything about them; they had almost disappeared into the city.

Charlie came over to the sofa with Jerry, the baby.

"Can I hold him?" I asked.

He handed him to me. I held him with his head against my shoulder, his face turned toward my neck. He fell asleep. He felt solid and warm.

I would have liked to ask Charlie what he thought about my holding his son so closely to me.

Charlie and Roberta sat on either side.

"What I keep wondering," I said, "is what impressions he's getting. In thirty years' time, if he wants to explain his life, he'll only be able to if he can remember this moment, which he won't be able to remember, because at this most important moment he's asleep."

Charlie said, "You should keep a record of it to show him in

52

thirty years."

"I'd like to keep a record of every single one of his impressions," I said.

This started Charlie off. He said he understood exactly what I meant – remembering your impressions was very important, not, though, to explain yourself, but as moments you live in terms of. He said he believed the Sacraments of the Church were important because they were vivid moments and you could always, later, look at those moments like fixed points, a constellation in the firmament of your life, and know you have had a life, all on a scale that surprised you, because you thought your life was unmemorable. The average person thought that. He, as an average person, certainly thought it about his life, until he remembered, say, his confirmation when the Bishop hit him on the cheek to startle him into the realities of the world.

Roberta said that was an argument for people to be baptized when they were old enough to remember it.

I said, "But surely Jerry wasn't baptized."

"We never considered the possibility," Charlie said.

"All of a sudden it seems odd to me," I said, "that our parents wouldn't ever have considered the possibility of our not being."

Charlie said it was amazing when you stopped and thought that Jerry's generation, brought up without religion, would find the iconography we were familiar with as foreign as that of oriental cults. Jerry would wonder what in God's name was going on in the pictures he'd see in museums and books: what was that person with wings saying to the young woman kneeling, and what was the radiating dove doing over her head? But he saw Roberta's point in not inculcating him with the imagery of a religion they no longer had faith in, imagery which, at best, would have abstract values, but no values for concrete life. Also, he thought, to bring up Jerry without the iconography of religion, leaving him, from Charlie's traditional Catholic point of view, with no imagery, would be an experiment; because if men needed images, Jerry would find them, would create them, and, if he had to create them, it would be interesting to see what they would be. But perhaps Jerry would show that

53

they weren't necessary, no more necessary, as Charlie himself had discovered, than belief in God, which his mother had thought essential to live. Charlie had proved his mother wrong, and maybe his son would prove him wrong, even though Charlie, as an artist, believed in the necessity of imagery. (He was now teaching drawing at a Catholic preparatory school.) Charlie related his life to images, and the strongest, he felt, were sacramental. But he had to admit it was possible that someone else, of another tradition, could lead a happy life without once revering even a photograph of his father. Anything was possible, which was what made the prospects of Jerry's future so exciting.

Jerry sighed, and moved a little in my arms.

Roberta listened to Charlie with more attention than I did, and it came to me, suddenly, that maybe she didn't think he was banal, but original, and if this were so, it was because she was, after all, less intelligent than he. Then I thought she made out in his talk original relationships of words and ideas I couldn't make out.

She said, "You're so funny, Charlie."

Among this family, I thought of my own family, my father and mother and their children, and I thought about the religious images of the Holy Family by which my family was assigned to certain ways of living. Everywhere in our small house images confronted us with the signs that, unless we lived in their terms, we were damned to have no relationships that would work. For us to have been a family fulfilled in the way a family was divinely meant to be fulfilled, my mother would have had to be a virgin, yet impregnated, not directly by the father of her son, but by a go-between, and that father not her husband; he, her husband, would have had to be the foster father of his wife's son, and to accept that, though his wife gave birth to a child, she remained a virgin, and he would have had to respect, throughout all their marriage, her virginity. And as for the son –

For those who believed, divine grace was so powerful it could transform a dead human body into a resurrected and glorified body that would exist forever in a world more real than this, but I wanted my life to be free of images that were fantasy. I insisted that the image of the risen Christ, his shroud a sheet flung from a body rising from the bed, must be expunged from the center of my thoughts and feelings.

Whenever I thought of those images in my family house, I thought of the house as a small cabin, and through the open windows and door of the cabin I looked out into woods, where, though I couldn't see them, I knew dark natives were moving about, looking towards the house through bushes and tangled vines.

While Roberta prepared a late lunch, I, sitting silently by Charlie with Jerry still in my arms, felt a restlessness beginning to take shape in me.

Jerry woke up, stared at me for a long time, wide-eyed, then his lower lip stretched over his gums, his eyes closed, and he cried. Saliva drooled down his chin. I tried to quieten him by bouncing him in my arms and saying "Gna, gna, gna," but he cried louder, and I had to give him to his father.

I thought, I could be a better father to him than Charlie.

"You'll just have to come more often," Charlie said, holding Jerry, now quiet, with one arm, and reaching out with the other to touch my shoulder.

Charlie's fatherhood made him sexless to me.

"Maybe I should come and live here," I said.

"That'd be great! That'd really be great!" He called out to Roberta, "Dan's going to come live with us!"

"Now that'd be interesting," she called back.

"I honestly do wish we could all live together," Charlie said.

With one hand, Roberta fed Jerry, on her lap, then fed herself, while she and I listened to Charlie talk about Jerry's future.

My restlessness deepened.

Charlie would interrupt himself often to say, "This is really good cooking, Roberta."

Suddenly, I thought I would have to get up from the table and walk around the room.

And just as suddenly, I felt that I was very heavy and couldn't move.

Roberta asked me, "Are you okay?"

55

I said, "I think I'm tired."

"All at once?"

My eyes flickered around her, but didn't fix on her. "I didn't sleep last night."

"What were you doing?" Charlie asked.

I looked at him and smiled. Roberta laughed first, then he did. They laughed, I thought, too much. Frightened, the baby began to cry. My eyes closed, I felt I could, sitting at the table, fall asleep. My eyes opened, I said, "I should go home."

"Don't go," Charlie said. "If you want to sleep, go lie on our bed."

"I've got to get back to my bed, because once I let go I'll probably be out for the night."

"Sleep here tonight."

Holding the baby over her shoulder and patting his back, Roberta waited for me to answer.

"It's been a joy to be here," I said, "a real joy, but now it's time to go because I can't take in any more joy or anything else. My senses have closed down for the day."

I kissed the top of the baby's head, then Roberta's cheek, and hugged Charlie before I left.

"You're really going back to your apartment?" Roberta asked.

"Sure," I said. "Why?"

"Well, you know you don't need to make excuses to us if you want to go somewhere else to see someone."

I kissed her again. "There's no one I want to see more than you," I said.

I leaned against the window of the streetcar. The vibrating glass shocked my skull. I sensed come over me, like sleep, the old, old possession of Charlie, and the old, old desire to possess that possession. Roberta possessed him.

Half asleep as I was, when I got out of the subway station, I thought I'd go, for five minutes, to the bar I'd been to the night before. The sun had set, but the air was light. Just for five minutes, I told myself.

There were not many people in the bar. I looked around at them, and stared, briefly, at one. Even if he had responded to me,

56

I wouldn't have been up to going out with him. I hadn't come to pick up anyone. It occurred to me why I'd come, why I came here again and again: to look, to keep renewing images. Maybe that was all I ever wanted here. I left after I finished my bottle of beer.

On my way to my room, through the deepening evening, a sense came over me that something had happened that had so changed me I'd always be different from what I'd been. But I didn't know what had changed me, or what the difference was.

I went to bed. I realized I'd forgotten what the person I'd spent the previous night with looked like, and I fell asleep trying to remember.

8

_____ • _____

One morning, when I stopped in the office to pick up my class forms, the proprietress, Mrs. Hart, gave me a letter which had been sent to me care of the school. I kept it unopened till the end of the day of lessons. The envelope didn't have the sender's address on it. After my last lesson, alone in the empty classroom, I opened the letter. It was from Henry, asking me to telephone him at home or at work.

He was at work. His voice was lower than I remembered it, low and steady. I expected him to be surprised that I called, but he wasn't. He said, "I won't be free until Saturday."

"All right," I said, and waited.

"Suppose you call me Saturday morning," he said.

"No," I said, "you call me, around ten, if you want."

He said he would, and hung up.

I told myself that he'd been brusque, but maybe that was because he was at work and couldn't talk. In my room, I read his letter once more, and thought, the fact was he was a brusque person, and the terseness of his writing had more to do with him in himself than the way he wanted to appear to me.

I felt powerful; and this sense of power over him disposed me to be warm towards him. The more I thought about it, the more warmly disposed I was towards him for having got in touch, and the more strongly my desire to impose myself upon him was replaced by the desire for him to impose on me.

He telephoned at ten o'clock.

It was a bright, hot morning.

"You come here, then we'll decide what we'll do," he said.

"Anything you want," I said.

Henry came to the door with a book closed over a finger. He was wearing chinos and a dress shirt, unbuttoned and out of his trousers, and he was barefoot. Holding out his free hand, he smiled; I took his hand and leaned towards him to kiss him, but I felt his arm was rigid, and I stood back.

He said, "Come on in."

He'd been reading in an armchair. On the floor around the chair were notebooks, looseleaf papers, pencils, eyeglasses. The living room smelled of dust. He sat back in the armchair and rested the book on a knee, his finger still inserted between the pages, as if, after a pause, he was going to resume reading.

I sat on the sofa, a little angry, as if all my affection towards him had been turned back on me.

He asked, "What would you like to do?"

I laughed.

He laughed also and closed the book and threw it on the floor, then leaned into the armchair.

I had to leave it to him.

He said, "I had an idea that we might go to L Street."

"L Street?"

"It's the old Boston beach."

"I'm sorry," I said, "I don't know it."

I didn't want to go to the beach. Maybe, I thought, I hadn't been forward enough in saying what I wanted to do, and he'd thought he shouldn't be more forward than I. So, neither of us wanting to, we were going to a beach. This seemed a waste of time.

In the car, I thought that maybe it was against Henry's way of doing things to make love during the middle of the day. I wanted, at any time, to make love as we had, but he, whose life was regulated by a different sense of right and wrong than mine, was only happy making love at night, or, perhaps, in the late afternoon. He was probably a person of many proprieties, none of which I knew. But this didn't mean that he was incapable of spontaneity. I thought that I knew everything there was to know

59

about his spontaneous feelings and thoughts, as he knew everything about mine. We had gone so far in our world, no other could matter.

Sitting side by side in the front seat of the little car, we began to talk about books. Henry was better read than I was, or he'd thought more about what he'd read. But I never felt at a loss to make a comment after he'd made one, and he took my comments more seriously than I gave them. I thought I was being mildly ironical. I hadn't often met someone who loved books, which was as embarrassing, in its way, as admitting you loved sex with men. I thought you had to be a little ironical about both. Not, I thought, that Henry could have been embarrassed about reading or liking sex with men, because his direct manner would always have made him say, without apology to anyone, I read books, I fuck men. He was not a person who had to justify himself. I was. With others, I had to justify my reading, and I had to justify my sex. With Henry, however, I didn't. He would have been considered by my home parish as affected, affected in his language as much as in his interests, but I realized he was, in fact, totally unaffected. He was able to express himself with total confidence, without once using a slangy word or phrase or changing his tone to one of even slight self-mockery. I liked it when he said, in his deep voice, "I'm of the opinion that – " He had the authority to do this, and his authority was sustained as much by his voice as by his face, which no one would have taken to be that of a weirdo reader of books.

We were now undressing in the locker room of the L Street clubhouse. Still talking about books, we went out onto the beach. I had a towel over my shoulders. Walking ahead of him, I pulled off the towel, and as I turned to him to respond to something he'd said, I saw him look at my body, then look away.

The sky, the ocean, the beach, even the buildings backing the beach made me feel more naked than I'd ever been, and the air around me, too, seemed to magnify my nakedness, as I walked across the sand behind Henry to a spot not far from the changing room. We spread towels and lay on them. We were among other naked men lying on the sand. Henry turned over on his stomach and closed his eyes, as if he had come here to sleep. I, propped on my elbows, looked around.

A group of boys were throwing a medicine ball to one another. They jumped about in the sunlight. Perhaps they were a familiar sight to Henry, but to me they represented a culture I knew nothing about. I had never, before I'd met Henry, known an authentic New Englander, though I was born and brought up in New England. My childhood friends, my high school and college friends, had all been Irish, Italian, Polish, all Catholic.

Oddly, I did not sense an air of rank sex among so many men naked together. Unlike me, a Catholic brought up to hide his body and to believe the naked body was always the occasion of sin, these people were brought up to believe that the naked body was nothing to be ashamed of: it was God-given, I thought. And what was mine? The naked body did not, for them, reflect sensuality, but health. I understood that this club had been instituted for the athletic body, which was chaste. If sensuality came upon it, the body should withdraw from public; but the body in itself was pure. Henry, here, seemed to have no awareness that he was among men who, simply by being naked, were in a state which couldn't be taken for granted, but had to astound. He slept.

I looked at his glistening body. Sand adhered to his calf and thigh. He came here often enough to be completely tanned. Perhaps he'd come as a boy, brought by his father, and he and his father had thrown a medicine ball to one another. As I always saw people in terms of their cultures I saw Henry now as an Old New Englander, and everything he said and did I'd interpret as an expression of that. Maybe because I'd never known any Yankees, I had strong preconceptions of what they were really like, and I was already attributing to Henry characteristics which he probably didn't have. He was supposed to be exclusive. He had asked me to come here. I wondered if he'd ever ask me into more private places. I was sure the Yankees had to lead lives unlike the one I'd led in New England, and unlike, too, those I'd assumed they led.

After a short time, he woke up and turned over onto his back.

61

He lay with his eyes open. All the fine hairs on his arms, nape, buttocks, legs were brilliant, and glowed about his body.

I asked, "Do you come here a lot?"

"Yes," he answered.

He didn't seem to want to talk now. He was so terse I wondered if I'd said or done something that had offended him. But I couldn't think what, and I decided he was just being himself, though I didn't know him in himself.

I thought he had to be aware that we were lovers.

Forget it, I said to myself. If he's not interested in you, you're not, after all, that interested in him.

Henry's Yankee body appeared perfect to me. That was what made it New England: it was perfect. There was not one detail, not a toe or a ball or a nipple or an eyebrow that was not ideal. His skin was clear, his limbs, his thighs, his chest, his shoulders, his head were finely proportioned, and I imagined his bones and muscles and blood and bowels as specimens of the body at its peak. And though someone might have said this body was characterless for not having one small disfigurement, it was just that characterlessness I liked about it: the body itself was the perfect outer personality of someone who perhaps didn't have a personality, or whose personality didn't matter. I knew I was making all this up. His body was not perfect.

I wondered what I looked like to him. He never seemed to look at me. Maybe, when I momentarily turned away, he did, but I never caught him.

In front of me, leaning against a brick wall, was a middle-aged man talking to an old man. The old, wrinkled man wore a cache-sexe. The middle-aged man had a large, powerful body, and his dark genitals hung heavily. I caught Henry looking at him at the same time I did, and he turned away. Immediately, I tried to dissemble my embarrassment by being ironical in a way I thought he would like.

I said, "I wonder what Walt Whitman would make of this beach."

Henry said, "Most every time I come here, I think of Whitman." He smiled at me. "How peculiar that you mentioned

62

him."

He was serious, and this moved me.

I thought no one else on the beach knew that we, two comrades, had made love. That was our secret among men, who were not supposed to make love. And the secret made us a couple. But perhaps everyone could see that we were a couple, that we had gone so far in our love making that the secrets which had been revealed to us had turned us into more than blood brothers. We were blessed as loving comrades by the blessing of our nation's greatest poet.

While Henry was talking, I wondered if my love for him was derived from some precedent he might be able to explain to me. I myself knew no precedent, and in my ignorance assumed my love was not derived from anything but the immediate body of Henry. And yet, as he talked about Whitman, I became nostalgic about the poetry I had not read at any length since my freshman year in college, nostalgic for what Whitman himself was so drawn to creating images of: the naked, perfect body.

His image of it was so fantastic, I wondered if he had ever made love with anyone.

Reading him, I had sometimes stopped with the sudden suspicion that he was an old faker. He was the greatest fantasy poet ever.

The miracle of Walt Whitman was that the self-consciousness, which he had to such a depth and height that it extended into the whole universe and beyond, did not condemn him and the universe, but made him exult in himself and the universes outside his universe. It was not out of some lack of un-self-consciousness that he was able to express the perfect body, the pure and natural body, with such passion, but because his self-consciousness went so far, went so high and so deep. It was what survived his self-consciousness, what he couldn't talk about, what he knew was pure and natural because he couldn't talk about it, that made him passionate.

The beach I was on was derived from Walt Whitman, and on it I felt, for a moment, love for all men, for all men and for all women, for everyone.

Whitman had written about himself and his poetry as he'd walked along a beach by the ocean:

O baffl'd, balk'd, bent to the very earth,
Oppress'd with myself that I have dared to open my mouth,
Aware now that amid all that blab whose echoes recoil upon
    me I have not once had the least idea who or what I am,
But that before all my arrogant poems the real Me stands
    yet untouch'd, untold, altogether unreach'd,
Withdrawn far, mocking me with mock-congratulatory
    signs and bows,
With peals of distant ironical laughter at every word I have
    written,
Pointing in silence to these songs, and then to the sand
    beneath. —

I understood what Whitman meant when he wrote, " . . . it is not for what I have put into it that I have written this book." What saved him, and what, at that moment on the beach, saved me, saved our entire country from thinking mockingly about ourselves, was his and my and our belief that there was something beyond the most extreme self-consciousness. "The words of my book nothing, the drift of it everything." He believed that everything appeared of itself in the vastness of his work, a vastness that was vaster even than his self-contradicting ego. It had so little to do with what he could intend, this everything he loved, that he thought it might come to him only with death.

I imagined that if I, lying by Henry in the sunlight, had died of my love for him, I would have had everything.

I did not, with Henry, feel that I was a fool.

Those images I saw about me – because I saw images of men rather than the men themselves – of men with sheer waists and massive arms, sunburnt, glistening with wet, little streams passing all over their bodies, men floating on their backs in the green water with their white bellies bulging to the sun, young men sousing one another with spray, struck me as if I had, just

64

then, seen what no one else had ever seen before, not even Walt Whitman.

I avoided looking at the physical deformities of the men, but if my attention fixed, for some reason, on a birth mark or a twisted leg, I thought: These, too, are natural, and in their way pure. There was no good and no bad. There was simply everything.

At the same time I was vaguely considering all this, I was thinking that, in fact, I was not in any kind of special place, and that I'd have preferred to be alone, back in my room, to do what I wanted to do, though I didn't know what that was.

I did not really like to be out in athletic America, but always wished I were in my small Catholic room, which was quiet.

I was made a little restless by Henry's talk.

I wanted to kiss his shoulder.

Our love making had given me certain rights of possession over him that he couldn't deny me. He was beautiful, and we were, together, beautiful. His having been in bed with me made me as beautiful as he was, because he wouldn't have gone to bed with anyone less beautiful than himself. Lying close to one another on the beach, we were more beautiful together than we were singly, and what drew us together was sex. So our sex, according to some syllogistic rule I'd long lost grasp of (all A is B, all B is C, therefore −), was beautiful. Henry had to be impressed, as I was, that because we had made love together once, we would make love again and again.

I turned more to face him, but he got up and said, "I'm going in for a swim." It was as if I wasn't allowed to go with him.

He didn't come back for a long while, and I went to where the grey waves broke into foam. Unable to see him, I went in deeper and swam up and down. When I returned to our towels, he was drying himself.

"I think we should go now," he said.

9

—— • ——

As we drove into Back Bay, our talk about the nude kept open the promised sex between us. But Henry could see the nude denuded of sex, as, say, an object of history. He was deeply interested in history (I wasn't really) and he talked mostly of poems, plays, novels from the point of view of the periods in which they were written (I regarded them as transcending all periods). I couldn't deny that his approach was probably better, because less sentimental, as a valid appreciation of literature; my approach left literature inexplicable, which was not an intelligent appreciation, but an ecstatic one. With him, I was absolutely sure that my approach was wrong and implied defective intelligence, while his approach, filled with intelligence, was right. But while I admired him, I wished he were able to detach himself, just a little, from his sense of serious study, which was, to him, work, and take me up for trying to be funny about it – especially now, when I wanted to bring it all down from the sky into our laps, to resolve it into fucking. But maybe Henry was ashamed to talk about sex.

Then I thought: he doesn't allow himself to say anything, to do anything, that is in any way self-conscious.

I reached out and grabbed his thigh and squeezed it, digging my fingers into it.

"Be careful," he said quietly, "or we'll have an accident."

I took my hand away.

Everything is going to be all right, I said to myself, you'll see, everything is going to be fine.

I let my body go loose, tilted my head back, and closed my eyes. My skin was tingling with sunburn and dried sea salt. If, for now, I couldn't touch him because it was dangerous, I could, in anticipation of touching him later, touch myself, and I slipped my hand under my tee-shirt.

You'll get everything you want, I thought.

Then this event took place: I felt myself thrown off-center and pulled to the side, and when I opened my eyes, I saw the maple trees along the street, lawns, porches all pass as the car, with a long screech, swung round. I went rigid, and even when the car stopped, facing the opposite way, I felt some continuing momentum would make the car inevitably crash, and I waited for the impact. I knew what it would be like. I felt that it was about to occur, and I reached out to hold Henry. My arms went round the motionless body leaning slumped against the steering wheel. Henry's eyes were open and staring.

I tried to pull him towards me. He turned only his head to look at me, though he seemed, too, to look through me. I said, "Henry." He asked in a low voice, "Yes?" "Are you all right?" "Yes," he went on in the same low, still voice, "I'm all right." There was no traffic in the sunlit street. We sat for a while longer, then Henry turned around and continued.

In silence, we drove into Back Bay. Students were lounging on the stoops and stairs of the brownstone houses. Henry stopped in front of the house where I lived.

Before I could say anything, he said, "I've been thinking I should go back to my apartment and work."

"Right," I said. But I didn't move, half thinking: this isn't everything. I opened the car door. "Thanks," I said.

He nodded.

I got out of the car and held the door open, then shut it when he went into gear.

I was twenty-four years old and I had studied myself in different circumstances enough to recognize the outward signs of my reactions to happenings. On the sidewalk, I saw in the many details – a crack in the cement, a popsicle stick – that what was happening inside me had happened before. I didn't want it to

67

happen again. The details held me for a while. I shook my head and looked into the distance, where the heavy sunlight blurred. Then I went up to my room. I stared at the map of Boston tacked to a wall.

What happened? I asked myself.

Look, I told myself sternly, whatever happened was entirely to do with him and had nothing to do with you. You said nothing, did nothing to make him leave you standing alone on the sidewalk the way he did. Nothing. And yet I kept asking myself, What happened?

Put it out of your mind, I thought. Without too much difficulty, you can put it out of your mind. Put what? Never mind what. Just stop thinking about it. About what? Stop it, now. Stop it? Yes, now.

I decided I'd be active. Lying on my bed, I thought a lot about being active.

The sunlight was flashing through a tree outside my window and into my room.

I got up and had a shower, then, drying myself with a towel, I wandered around my room thinking, You've got to go out and do something. You can't stay in.

Then I thought I wanted to be with Roberta. Not with Charlie, too. With her alone. I knew so little about her experience in the world, but I felt she would be able to tell me what to do because she seemed to be a person of greater experience than I.

I telephoned her, but there was no answer.

In clean clothes, I went out. I went to the Charles River Esplanade and walked along it, sometimes stopping to study the sailing boats in the bay.

When I found myself staring at a boy lying on the grass, I realized I had been staring at him with no sense of why I was, as if I could have no reason.

Although it seemed to me I was out for hours, not even an hour went by before I returned to my room. And there I would, after a short time, want to go out again.

This time Charlie answered the phone.

"I thought we might get together," I said.

"I'm taking care of Jerry while Roberta's out working in the library," he said. "Come on over. We can fool around with Jerry on the lawn in the back yard."

In the back yard, we sat and drank beer while Jerry crawled on the grass.

The fact was, I didn't want to be with Charlie.

He talked and, from time to time, got up to stop Jerry putting grass blades or sticks or pebbles into his mouth. I tried to pay attention to Charlie. I even asked questions, though I wasn't sure if they related to what he was saying. I drank a lot of beer, thinking that would give me some control. As often as I said to myself, you can't let it happen, you've got to do something so it won't happen, something like the round rim of my beer can would assert that it was happening and there was nothing I could do about it. All that would be left of me would be some thin, peripheral perception of details.

The father picked up his son and jogged around the yard with him. I would soon imagine that there was nothing in their relationship, that, at best, Charlie was pretending to be a father (which was a suspicion I always had anyway) and that Jerry, in his infantile way, was pretending to act as a laughing son (an entirely new suspicion). Soon, it would seem to me that nothing ever happened between them that could make any difference to one or the other. That was not true, of course. Everything they did to one another made a difference to them. But in a while I wouldn't think it did. I looked at a little black and blue mark on Jerry's forehead, and a similar mark on Charlie's neck, and these seemed to me of more interest than their playing together. Their playing together not only bored me, I began to be irritated by it, by its pretentiousness. Charlie really was a phony. He always had been, and he always would be. Even as a father, he was a phony.

"Haven't you played enough with him?" I asked.

"You're jealous," he said. "You wish I were playing with you like this."

He went on playing. I got up and went into the apartment and walked around.

69

I wished I could go back to Charlie and say, Look, something terrible is happening, and you've got to help me stop it.

Roberta came in and found me walking up and down the living room.

"Where're Charlie and Jerry?" she asked.

"Outside."

"Is anything wrong?"

"Why should anything be wrong?"

"What're you doing in here while they're out there?"

I shrugged.

Charlie came into the living room carrying Jerry. He said to Roberta, "Dan telephoned and told me he was restless, so I told him he should come on over to us. Isn't it great that he telephoned us when he was restless and wanted to see people?"

She asked me, "What's making you restless?"

"I don't know," I answered. "It just comes over me."

I was frightened to be on my own, but, while we were eating supper, I realized I had no less reason for being frightened among this family. They were not going to stop what was going to happen; they couldn't. I began to imagine it was more dangerous for me to be among them than to be alone, because they were a family, and as a family all their relationships were fixed and everything they said and did was predictable. I sensed that among them nothing could be different.

I thought, looking at Charlie: I could show you a time you've never even dreamed of.

I said, trying to laugh, "Don't you two ever get bored being a family?"

"Bored?" Charlie asked.

Roberta said, "Of course we get bored." As I'd seen her do over and over, she was feeding the baby from a bowl next to her plate. She dipped the spoon into the mush, then scraped it against the rim of the bowl.

An edge came into my voice. "I'm sure I'd end up killing the baby."

Charlie said, "Oh, come on."

"Sometimes," I said, "I think they're aware of what ego-

70

monsters they are, aware that they can get away with demanding everything just because we believe they're helplessly unaware."

Charlie said to me, "Dan, we look forward to the day when he's grown up and we can give you the same attention."

I came away thinking I had to sustain my sense of possibilities by going to the bar by the bus station.

It seemed to me that Henry had, after leaving me, disappeared and could not have any presence anywhere. When I saw him at the back of the bar I wondered who this person was. He was talking with another man. I didn't know if he saw me or not. I turned away.

It annoyed me, even angered me, that he existed, because he should have been so dependent on my imagining him that he could only exist because I did imagine him. He could exist only if I allowed him to, and if, suddenly, I decided I didn't want him to, he would disappear. I was especially angry to see him wearing a foulard tucked into his open collar, which I would never have imagined him wearing and therefore never allowed him to wear. He should have asked my permission to dress as he did, to eat what he did, to shit, to sleep, to say what he said. He didn't. He did what he wanted.

I went to a wall and leaned against it and drank my beer.

He came to me. "I thought I'd take a little break from work," he said.

"You don't have to excuse yourself to me."

"No."

"It was a nice afternoon," I said.

He held out his hand, and I shook it. He left the bar and I finished my beer, then left.

In my room, as I stood by my bed, I imagined there appeared over my head a halo, not of gold, but of black iron.

I undressed.

I found myself thinking there was something I should be considering, but it was not anything that could come from thinking.

It came to me: the image of Henry lying on his bed, asleep. This image took possession of me.

71

10

————— • —————

What happened to me could only be explained, I thought, by my being a Catholic. There was no way I could tell Henry this. He would find my explanation ridiculous. And so it was.

As a Catholic, I felt my childhood had, in a way that seemed simultaneously concrete and elusive, been like that night I'd spent with Henry: there was no explaining it, there was only experiencing it, like some strange conversion, to have any sense of it. I was born and brought up in the Mystical Body. This was as real a body of flesh and blood, I, taking off from dogma, imagined, as the body of someone I loved. The Church I was a part of lay on the earth, its arms and legs wide, its head thrown back, and Christ loved this body. Every time people made love, they re-enacted in their love act the mystical love of Christ for his Church. At the end of the world, this body would rise, glorified and immortal, made of the millions of bodies of the glorified and immortal members of the corporeal Church, and Christ and this gigantic body would be, forever, lovers. In my Church, to deny your body was to deny your soul.

No one could take this seriously.

I didn't take it seriously. But I understood, and I was suspicious that I was using my religion to explain my ridiculous obsession by a body denied me. I was using, or trying to use, my religion not only to explain, but to excuse the sense of my ridiculousness. Of course, of course, my obsession was ridiculous. So was my religion.

Henry knew how ridiculous it was.

What bewildered, what angered me most was that he had got in touch with me, not I with him. What had he expected?

And what had made him turn away from me? He didn't know me, as I didn't know him. Whatever it was that had turned him against me couldn't have had to do with my personality. What was wrong with my body that he had seen it, naked in the sunlight, as repellent to him? If he had denied me his body, I, in my body, had repelled him, had made him deny me. It was all the fault of my body.

While I taught my students, I imagined that we weren't dealing with the real subject of the lessons. In every composition I read, not the absence, but the presence of the absence of Henry.

A young South American student, my first for the day, gave me his composition.

My problems in English
I have seven day of live in Boston city. This has for object
to correct my problems and to desire very much outcomes.
The End

I thought, I will never be able to correct his language any more than I'll be able to put right what I did wrong. And yet, there was no question but that I had to.

As I thought out, with effort, explanations for the simplest and yet most complicated mistakes, I tried, at that level deeper than the compositions, to explain what it was about me that made Henry not want to see me.

I told myself there was nothing shocking about Henry's not wanting to make love with me again. He had not been powerfully moved by it, as I had. To him, it was no more important, maybe less important, than a casual conversation about, say, Boston. He would have been puzzled, angered too, to know how important it had been to me. The more I considered the image of him, however, the more important the image became, meaning everything I wanted and couldn't have. I was no one for not being able to have what it promised. I was shocked by his denial of me.

As I sat at the classroom table during a short break, there came to me, as if I had for a fraction been distracted, the sudden suspicion that I was not looking at his image. I closed my eyes. I saw, not a whole body, but an ankle, an elbow, a featureless face. I saw, as hard as I tried, nothing whole. And yet, the sense was of something utterly whole. But what did this sense rely on?

I could have gone through the class hours haphazardly, or I could have gone down to Mrs. Hart and said I wasn't well and had to leave for the rest of the day, but I never thought to.

In the end, the strain I felt was like having to correct, all over again, what I still believed was impossible to correct, though I'd done it. In the waning afternoon, as I sat alone in the classroom after I'd filled out the register, I thought that I must correct not only what made me wrong according to Henry but what made me wrong on earth.

Drawing circles, squares, triangles on a sheet of paper I asked myself, what *is* wrong with me? My mind stopped.

In the next room, I heard a lesson going on. The teacher was saying, "No, not snows. It snows."

"It?"

"Yes, it snows."

"What is it that snows?"

"What is it?"

"Yes." There was a silence, and after a while the teacher said, "It. You don't understand?"

I thought: I don't understand –

I stopped.

What sin I committed –

You know, you know, a voice said. You wanted everything. You only thought of yourself. That's what's wrong with you. You only ever think of yourself, and you know that's a sin. You are in a constant state of sin. You are, in the very fact that you are yourself, embodied sin. Your body is a sin. Your –

Don't be stupid, I said. I don't believe in sin.

The voice laughed. And what else don't you believe in? it asked.

I concentrated on the geometrical figures I was drawing to try

74

to think of nothing else, and I wished these figures were all I ever thought.

I don't believe in anything, I said.

The high, thin voice said, It doesn't matter now if you believe or not, your beliefs are with you whether you want them or not. You believe you are a sin.

I don't, I said, and pressed my pencil to make a heavy line.

The voice said, You do.

Maybe, I thought, I'm not possessed. Maybe I only imagine I am, and, with the smallest effort of will, I could dispossess myself. I should do this, should exert this smallest effort of will.

I drew a circle.

The voice said, But maybe you need to feel you are possessed. Maybe your need is such that even if you have to invent the possession, you'll do it to imagine you're possessed. Maybe it's only when you feel you are possessed that you're in a state of –

I drew a square.

The voice: Grace. A state of grace. That's what possession is for you.

I: But I don't want to be possessed. I want to get rid of my possession.

The voice: You don't.

I: I do.

The voice: You don't. You want the possession.

I said, For Christ's sake, if you had any religious training, you'd know you can't be possessed by grace and in a state of sin at the same time.

The voice, high and thin, said, Don't tell me I don't know religion. Of course you're in a state of sin. You'll always be in a state of sin. But your possession is the longing to be in the state of grace. And I suspect that's the closest you'll ever come to grace.

I put my hand up to my forehead and closed my eyes to try to see in my mind simple squares, circles, triangles.

I am possessed by him, I thought, I am possessed by him, I am possessed –

Another voice, low and thick, said, No, you're not.

I am, I said. I haven't invented the possession. I am possessed.

75

No, the voice said. You could stop it, with the slightest act of will. But you don't want to.

I can't stop it. I can't.

You want to remain in a state of sin.

I opened my eyes and stared at the geometrical figures on the piece of paper. I said, All right, I'll stop the possession, I'll make the act of will, I'll – I tried to think of only the asymmetrically drawn figures.

The lesson in the next room finished. The teacher and the student went out and the building sounded empty when I heard a door downstairs shut.

A third voice, that of a young woman, almost a girl, asked: But why are you possessed by something that has been taken away from you?

What? I asked.

She said, I can understand being possessed by something you're given, but not by something taken away. Why are you possessed by what is denied to you?

I have to think, I said.

You're not very good at thinking, she said.

Let me think.

The thin, high voice said, Maybe you can only ever be possessed by what you can't have.

The girl asked, But why?

Because he can only ever want, never have.

The heavy, low voice asked, But why?

The girl said, That's what I want to know. Why?

I said, I don't want to listen to this talk about me. I don't want to hear about myself, don't want to think about myself.

I hit my forehead.

The voice of an old man whispered, What do you want?

Lowering my head to the table top, I said, I want not to think about what I want. I want not to think about myself. Help me not to think about what I want, about myself and my wants. Help me do that.

We can't, the old man said.

Can't you talk about something else? I asked. Can't you try?

The old man's voice: You wouldn't be interested in anything else.

I sat up. I said, I'm not possessed. I'm imagining I am. I can stop it at any moment.

The girl's voice: Then stop it.

I'll stop it.

We're waiting, the old man said.

Instead of talking about me, I said, why don't we talk about the outside world? There's a lot going on in the outside world, a lot that's very interesting. There must be a war going on somewhere. We could talk about that. Or a famine. Or unemployment. Or, if you want, we could talk about other people. Other people are interesting.

You're not interested, the old man said.

I am.

You're not, the girl said.

I am. I am.

The high and low voices said, together: You can only think about yourself.

Fuck off, I said. Out loud, I said, "Fuck off."

I threw the paper with the geometrical drawings into the wastepaper basket, then went out.

In the office downstairs, Mrs. Hart asked me about the Panamanian student.

"I wonder," I said, "if he's hopeless."

"You can't have that attitude and teach," she said. "No one can ever be hopeless."

She had no sense of humor.

All right, I thought as I walked through Back Bay. Someone wants to ask me a question.

I heard the girl's voice say, Are you prepared?

Ask it.

Listen carefully.

I'm listening.

There was a pause. I've forgotten it, she said.

I'm waiting impatiently.

I'm trying to think of it.

Come on.

Your impatience is making it difficult for me to concentrate.

Come on.

Here it is. Now listen. I'll say it slowly.

Come on.

What is it you want from him that he won't give you?

That's a question I can't answer.

You should be able to answer any question.

Should be?

Well, why not? If you did a little more thinking, real thinking, you'd probably be able to answer. But I know you. You don't like thinking, not like I do. All questions can be answered if you think hard enough.

Maybe I should ask you a question or two, I said, as you think so hard.

It may take me time to answer, and you're impatient.

I'll give you the time.

Then ask me a question, any question.

What do I want from him that he won't give me?

She laughed.

I said, I don't want anything from him. Nothing.

But you do, the old man said. You want his –

Stop it, I said, stop it.

He laughed.

I said, You're right to laugh. You're all right to laugh.

The girl said, You want his –

Laughing more, the old man said, His heart.

All I want, I said, is to stop this.

The woman said, Oh, his big, bleeding heart–

Stop it, I said.

Oh, his thorn-tangled heart, dripping with blood, the old man said.

If you won't stop it, I said, go on, go on. Make it a joke. That's fine with me.

Oh, the girl said, his scourged, nailed, speared heart–

Go on, I said. Exaggerate.

His bleeding heart, that would bless you with grace if only he

78

would give it to you–

Exaggerate more, I said. Exaggerate.

I heard another voice, that of a woman and a man combined. It said, No, we're going to take you very seriously.

Shocked by this voice, I thought, I am going to think this out on my own, and, once it's thought out, I'll be able to see it, like a geometrical figure. I'm going to be logical. My premise is: A) that I want to be dispossessed of him. B) If I want to be dispossessed of him, I don't want anything from him. C) If I don't want anything from him, I have no reason to think about him. D) If I think about him without having a reason to, I think about him unreasonably. E) Unreasonable thinking is not true thinking. F) I do not think about him. G) If I do not really think about him, he doesn't truly exist for me. H) If he doesn't truly exist for me, I can't want him. I) I don't want him –

I unlocked the street door to the house and climbed the wooden stairs. I locked the door to my room behind me. I threw school papers onto my desk. Sweating, I pulled off my clothes and went into the bathroom. As I stepped into the old, claw-footed tub to draw the shower curtain around it, I caught sight of my body in the mirror on the back of the bathroom door.

I thought it was an attractive body.

I said to myself, If I knew what is wrong with me that keeps him from wanting to see me, and if I put that wrong right, he'd want to see me.

You can't make what's wrong right, someone said. It's not possible by thinking about yourself.

What's wrong about you can be made right only by thinking of someone else, another voice said. You've got to think of someone else.

But I only think of someone else, I shouted.

No –

Yes. And I will devote my life to thinking about him. I will make him want me. I will think of nothing else, devising ways, with all the subtlety of someone devising strange meetings and relationships, to get him to long for me. I can do it. I'm French. And not just long for me. Long for me to fuck him – in the

79

mouth, the nose, the ears, and oh up the ass, again and again up the ass – all the while saying, More. He had to want me, he had to want to make love with me again. How, after our love making, could he not want to? I would make him long for my sinful body.

He'll want me, I thought, and I'll have him, and then I won't ever want him again.

The semen on my fingers gummed in the hot water and I had to scrape it off with my nails.

I dried myself and sat in an old arm chair, the towel wrapped about my waist, and tried to read a student's composition.

I heard another voice. It was the voice of a terrifying queen. He said, You!

I sat still.

His voice rose to a screech when he said, Pay attention to me.

I lowered the composition, then remained still again.

We want to examine you, he said.

There was faint laughter.

He said, Everything about you is wrong. Everything.

The laughter became louder.

No wonder he doesn't want you, the queen said.

Fuck off, I said.

The voice trilled as it screeched. Fuck off? it exclaimed. Fuck off?

Yes.

I listened.

I'm not going to think about what I want, I said. I'm not going to.

I listened again.

I don't long for anything, I shouted.

I stood in the silence, and swung my arms.

What do I want? I said. What do I want? For Christ's sake, can't everyone see? It's not grace. No, no. It's nothing as high as that. All I want is his low body.

I went to a wall and leaned my forehead against it and pushed with my weight.

His body was mine, and it was taken away from me. Why, now, was I possessed by what was taken away from me?

80

I hit the wall.

I am going to make him want to make love. I am going to make him long for it, as with a longing for salvation. I'm going to make him wish he had never met me.

11

———— • ————

It seemed to me the day had been a night, and I had been asleep, and now that it was night, I sat at my desk and woke up.

I wanted to be – and I was amazed when the word came to me in my appeal for a word – free. I would not be able to love anyone, not know anyone, unless I was free, and to be free was to apprehend the world as it was, to apprehend even objects – a shoe, a sock, underpants on the floor – as they were.

To be free, I told myself, was to be without intentions. To be free was to be large and open, to be universally accepting, and, in the midst of such large openness, to allow objects in themselves to occur to you without trying to make them what they weren't. I must learn, I thought, I must learn not to impose myself on things. I have always tried to impose myself on things, on people, on whole countries. I think I have tried to impose myself on the universe. I have imposed all my thinking and feeling on Henry to make him mine, something that should be mine, something I fantasized as mine and even as being myself. I must not do this, though it may mean that I must stop thinking and feeling altogether. That was what I really wanted: to stop thinking and feeling altogether.

In my hatred, I imagined that if I hit my thigh and the side of my chest against an edge, his perfect body would fly out from me and disappear. All fantasy was impure, was sinful, I thought, and it was because it had nothing to do with the world. All my thoughts and feelings, fixed in fantasy, had nothing to do with the world.

And yet, how I was pulled with amazed wonder to the photograph, in a pornographic magazine, of a young man and a young woman making love.

What was the most hateful fantasy? It was of a body, but not anyone's body. It was of the ideal body. We all loved it for its wholeness which we didn't have. It did nothing, but it existed, and we referred our small particulars to it, or we would have if we could have found, by some process of collective intuition, its center. We wanted to believe the general could exist in itself, without the particular, if it had a center; for some reason we wanted to believe this, wanted to believe we could have, without having any one thing, everything in itself. We wanted the body at its most abstract, at its most whole, which was a secret kept from us by that brilliant body. This was the worst fantasy.

I told myself I must see someone I had no image of. I knew I wouldn't be able to sleep. Before it got too late, I thought I would call Roberta.

Charlie answered. "What are you up to?" he asked.

Suddenly, as I'd known would happen, I wondered why I had called. "Nothing. I was missing you."

"How about going out?" he asked. "I'll pick you up in my car."

"It's not too late?"

"I know some places where you and I can spend the night drinking if we want."

"I mean, for the family."

He held the receiver away from his face, but I heard him talking, I presumed, to Roberta.

She came on the line.

"You are family," she said.

When Charlie came back on the line, I said to him, almost as if it rose out of me like a pain, "I've got to talk to you," and immediately I laughed.

I was on the curb when he drove up, and he leaned over the passenger seat to open the door.

We went to a bar down by the wharves and sat in a booth and ordered bottles of beer. Charlie liked going to rough places. He

83

thought of himself, in some ways, as being rough, as having, he sometimes said, the soul of a truck driver.

He was waiting for me to tell him what I had to tell him, but Charlie wouldn't press. His way of not imposing on me was to talk himself, hardly with any expectation of my listening. Nodding, I hardly listened.

Smiling, he held his bottle of beer up to me and said, "You're not interested in what I have to say, but you wouldn't tell me that for the life of you."

"I like listening to you."

"You don't."

"I like listening to you talk, but it doesn't matter at all what you're talking about."

He laughed loud.

If I didn't tell him what I had to say, he'd feel that I was holding something back from him, and I didn't want him to feel that. But to tell him would be to exaggerate what I had no reason to think was important. In the unpainted wooden booth with him, drinking beer, I felt close to him. Though it would sound like an exaggeration, I'd still have to tell Charlie, because he was waiting. I couldn't remember ever having telephoned to tell him I had to talk to him. Across the table from me, he put his head against the high, straight back of his seat.

I said, "I've fallen in love."

"Who with?"

"It doesn't matter who with, because I'm the only one who's in love."

He drank beer and put the bottle down, then crossed his arms.

"I want you to tell me how I can get over it," I said. "I don't want to exaggerate. I'm not in any kind of desperate state. Don't think that. You know I'm not the kind of person who exaggerates. And you know I'm not the kind of person who imposes. I don't because, really, I never have any reason for imposing, not any reason important enough. This isn't important. You mustn't give it any importance."

He said, "If it isn't that important, you shouldn't have any trouble getting over it."

84

"It isn't important," I said, "but I can't get over it. It isn't greatly interesting to you, or Roberta, or anyone, not even to me, but there it is, and I can't get over it."

"Look," he said, "You come and spend the night with us."

"I can't impose."

"I'm going to impose on you."

"I'll pay for the beers," I said.

In the car, Charlie talked without stopping. I couldn't talk.

The apartment was dark.

I whispered to Charlie in the entrance hall. "I should go back to my room."

"You're staying here."

He switched on a light in the living room, and told me to wait while he went into his and Roberta's bedroom. I could hear them talk, her voice low. He came out with a blanket and a pillow.

"Roberta said she went to bed because she thought we'd be out late."

I used the bathroom after him, then undressed to my underpants, switched off the lamp, and lay on the sofa.

From their room, I heard Charlie and Roberta talking. They stopped.

The ceiling in the living room of the old tenement apartment was high.

I must sleep, I thought. I have to sleep.

But I couldn't, and I finally got up from the sofa to walk around the room.

I said, "What am I going to do?"

I was angry, but it took me a while, walking around the room, to figure out why. It was because Charlie and Roberta were asleep and I was awake. Half-intentionally, I stumbled and stomped hard with a foot. In their bedroom, the baby cried, and I heard Charlie and Roberta speak. One of them got out of bed to quiet the baby in his crib. I listened. After a long silence, I walked around the room again, hitting the floor with the heels of my feet. When I heard voices again from the bedroom, I lay on the sofa and covered myself with a blanket.

In the living room, Roberta said, "Dan?"

"Yes," I answered.

"Are you all right?"

"I'm sorry. I can't sleep."

She came to the sofa in her nightgown and sat at my feet. "Charlie told me what happened," she said. "I hope you don't mind that."

"No," I said. "I'm glad he told you. I wanted him to tell you." I folded my arms behind my head and could smell my own odor. "But I don't know what more to say."

"Maybe you feel you have too much to say."

"There's that."

"Who is he?"

"It's as if it doesn't matter who he is."

"You fell in love with him, and not just anyone. It does matter who he is."

"I fell in love with him because he wouldn't fall in love with me, no other reason."

"I see."

"No," I said, "there are other reasons. You're right. I fell in love with him and not just anyone, and that's because when he –" I stopped.

"What?"

"Nothing."

She said, after a moment, "I'll tell you what you should do."

"Oh?"

"Bring him here."

"Why?"

"Just so you'll be able to see him from the outside and recognize he's not as ideal as you think."

"From a scientifically analytical point of view," I said, "it's interesting, isn't it, that when you are in love with someone you go into a state of finding him ideal. It's a very distinct state of awareness."

I could see Roberta in the dimness smiling at me.

"You see," I said, "I'm not completely without awareness."

"I never thought you were," she said.

It seemed to me that, given the time, I could explain

everything to Roberta by making subtle connections among the flashing ideas in my head, so they would be resolved into a whole. She expected me to be very clear-headed. I said, "I sometimes believe the sense of wonder implies a state of mind as distinct as the most logical conclusion to a syllogism."

Her smile widened. I wondered if she was going to say, "You're funny – "

"At moments, while you're making love, and, all at once, you see your lover's face, you feel – "

"But – " she began.

I couldn't allow her to break in on my connections. "Suspicious as I always am of wonder, that moment of wonder, I allow myself to – " The connections were breaking. I spoke quickly. "I have to allow that, as a distant state, it has – That if it, in itself, survives my suspicions that it is false, is corrupt, what remains of it – " I stopped. "It's all broken down."

"You haven't told me a word about him."

"I can't."

"Try."

"He has a nice apartment. He works in a library, where he can't earn much, but maybe he doesn't have to earn much."

She grunted.

I said, "Why am I not at all, but not at all, interested in his life?"

"It'd help if you were."

"I see that. But, still, why aren't I interested?"

"You're asking an impossible question."

"Has anyone ever made a study on lapsed Catholics?" I asked.

Roberta yawned. "You think it's as a lapsed Catholic that you've reacted to this guy?"

"You're very good at being interested."

"I have to be whether I want to or not."

I said, "My getting in touch with Henry to invite him here would be false, because I would be doing it for some selfish intention. If he, however, telephoned me and asked me if he could come, I would believe that wasn't false, because that would have nothing to do with my intending it. He'd know I was trying to get him to react for my sake, to get something from him. He has to telephone me."

"You telephone him and invite him."

"He won't come."

"Maybe he will."

"I know I'd feel completely false calling him up to invite him."

"Then bear yourself feeling false."

"I do. I do. I do that all the time. I bear my being false, and I do what I have to do. I'm a fake as a teacher, but I do teach, and well, I think. I'm a fake as a reader of books and as a looker at pictures and as a listener to music, but I do these well, too. I'm pretty sure I'm a fake being a friend, but I hope I'm good at it. And I will not allow myself to become cynical. Mildly ironical, maybe, but not cynical."

"You'll be very good at calling him up and asking him to come here."

"It's as though you were imposing some terrible responsibility on me."

"That's exactly what I want to do."

"I don't want to do it, Roberta."

"You do it."

I said, "You know, I have a very strong sense of responsibility. I really do. I keep telling myself, You're strong willed. It's odd, but I sometimes think it's this strong will that would make it possible for me to have a strong relationship with a woman. Yet, all the while, self-consciously, I keep wishing I could relinquish all my responsibility and make that simple act of faith by which I would be taken over by a will stronger than mine, and that would be a man's will."

"He's not going to call you," Roberta said, "if that's what you're praying for. You're going to call him."

"I can't. As a lapsed Catholic, I can't. I don't have the faith."

"Keep telling yourself, Tomorrow, I'm going to call him, tomorrow I'm going to speak to him, and you'll be all right, at least until you call him."

"The comfort of taking on responsibility –"

"It is a comfort," she said.

From the bedroom, Charlie called, "Roberta."

With a note of mockery that, in some way, pleased me, she said, "My husband's calling me," but she didn't move.

I said, "Here's a subject for a study: the Holy Family as a paradigm for the human family."

"Roberta," Charlie called.

12

———•———

Every time the image of Henry appeared to me in my sleep, I woke up.

A friend who was a psychologist once said to me that I could not possibly have the dream images I insisted that I did have, and still be able to sleep: I told him I had dreamt I'd made love with my mother and that my father cut off my balls with a straight razor. Such images, he said, would never be allowed to pass whatever it is in the mind that censors unbearable images. But they did come to me without my waking up, and I remembered them vividly. After what my friend told me, I imagined that I hadn't been so disturbed by the images that I woke shouting, because such images are so common we are not disturbed by them. I thought: either the very notions that arouse such images were themselves so exposed that we accepted them as a matter of course, or the most frank images of those notions had become irrelevant to the notions themselves.

I did not know what the image of Henry referred to, when it came to me in my sleep and woke me, but it frightened me.

I knew I'd be all right if I could sleep and really dream. That always helped me if I got into a distracted state. There had been a time in my life when I slept for fifteen hours a day, for day after day, and, afterwards I was all right.

But just asleep, suddenly free in the spacious freedom from thought, I would think, Shouldn't you be thinking about something? And just as I'd tell myself, No, no, don't think, I would, with the sensation of being joltingly caught up short, be brought back to the image.

I thought that I should try to think what the image of Henry meant to me that it kept me awake. Perhaps I could explain my obsession away. But this was like attempting to explain why the images that occurred of making love with your mother and being castrated by your father did not frighten you. The difficulty was not that my explanations of the frightening possession by the image of Henry were too complex, it was that they were too simple. Every meaning I came up with seemed in the end too simple.

What about Mère Ste Epiphane, in the parochial grammar school, saying that Christ's greatest suffering was not the flagellation, not the crowning of thorns, the carrying of the cross, the crucifixion, but his having to hang on the cross naked, his body entirely exposed to everyone?

My religion did not allow meanings outside itself, and in itself all its meanings were obvious.

I went through all the images, all the fantasies of my religion I could think of. They all struck me as irrelevant to anything but the most banal explanations of that image of Henry. In the same way as easy psychology could not be used to explain the most obvious of its images, so my religion could not be used to explain the image that frightened me because it possessed me. The real reasons for my possession and fear of the image surely were deeper than my religion. I believed, too, that they were deeper than the psychology of my particular personality, a personality completely determined by my religion.

In the dawn light, I heard the baby cry. I heard the consoling sounds of Roberta, who went into the kitchen with him. After a while, she returned with him to the bedroom.

I didn't want to speak to anyone. When Charlie came into the living room to say, "Dan," I pretended I was asleep. He came over to the sofa and touched my shoulder. "Dan," he said. I opened my eyes. In his underpants, he was standing over me and looking down at me.

"I thought you'd want to get ready to go to school," he said.

I licked my lips. "Thanks."

91

"How are you?"

"I'm fine."

Out of the bathroom, where I'd shaved with Charlie's razor, I dressed and folded the blanket on the sofa.

Charlie came in, dressed. "We'll have something to eat," he said, speaking softly. "Then I'll drive you."

"Thanks," I said, "but I'll go now."

"Dan –"

"It's all right. I'm all right. But I want to go now."

While I was waiting for the streetcar, it came to me that my perceptions had changed, that I was not seeing or hearing as I had been the day before. What I saw – the windshields of passing cars reflecting overhead trees, telephone posts and wires, the clear morning sky – was without dimension. It was as if some sense in me had ceased, some sense of dimension which had put me in the same space as what I saw. It took me a long time to figure out that things were visually disconnected from me because I had no visual awareness of space. Without space, objects existed in a baffling way, and perhaps my concentrated wonder about them was how they could exist so assertively, with hard, sharp edges, in no space.

I got on the trolley.

Something else, I knew, had happened which the visual flatness merely indicated: a break had occurred in my very appreciation of objects, so that nothing I thought about them applied. I fixed myself on them to try to make some kind of sense of them, but I couldn't. They kept their meaning to themselves. Never did I think they were without meaning. They were nothing but meaningful in themselves. But I was incapable of appreciating this, as incapable as I was of understanding how objects could exist in no space. They defied me by their own weird state of being, which frightened me.

As I was walking up the steps of the brownstone school I imagined I saw Henry standing still behind the glass in the wooden front door where the school's name appeared in gold letters, and a horror passed over me. I stopped on the steps. The door opened and a colleague came out, but the horror remained.

My colleague held the door open for me to go in.

I was horrified, but I was, at the same time, not at all interested in my horror.

My students' compositions were flat. I had to work against my complete lack of interest in them. Sometimes I wanted to say, Give up, it isn't worth it. And yet, their attempts to get the sentences right, both written and spoken, moved me. Something moved me that maybe had nothing to do with my students.

Often, I thought, you've got to telephone Henry.

In my room, I asked myself how I had got through the day.

You did it, a voice said.

Of course you did it. What happened that was so terrible you couldn't work? You think it's a reason not to work that someone doesn't want to fuck with you? What is this? Not fucking the person you want to fuck is going to change your life? Come off it. What you want isn't important enough to make you even think about not being able to work. Jerking off should take care of what you want. No, if you think you can't work, there has to be another reason. If you can't work, it won't be because of a non–fuck. But let me tell you, no reason is going to be enough to excuse you from working. You'll have to work, correcting your students' talk and writing, day after day, because nothing's going to excuse you. You hear?

Shut up, I said.

I got up and went to my desk and sat at it. The telephone was on a corner, on a book. This was just the moment to telephone Henry. I had to keep reminding myself of it, as if it were the least important thing I had to do that day.

At my desk, I conscientiously tried to devise images that would apply to my state of mind. All my concentration went into this, because I thought I must be able, somehow, to make a connection between a particular and an abstract state. I tried to do this because the split I had noticed that morning between my inward state and the outward world – the outward world being, now, nothing but flat images – had come between me and my image of Henry lying naked on his bed. I knew I would not be

93

able to make contact with what that image inspired.

The telephone rang. "Have you called him?" Roberta asked.

"I tried," I said, "but there was no answer."

"You'll try again, won't you?"

"Sure."

"You won't believe me if I tell you he isn't perfect, because no human being is. You'll say it's because I haven't met him. So let me meet him."

"I don't know if I should," I said, "if your intention is just to make me see his defects. Why should I see his defects?"

She shouted, "You've got to!"

I would have gone through day after day of the heaviest work rather than telephone him.

"All right," I shouted back, "I will."

I would do it after I ate. But even opening a can of soup and heating it on an electric ring seemed to me to require too much concentration, so I went out to a delicatessen and had a sandwich and a beer at a table on which the wipe marks of a rag had dried.

At the next table, I heard this conversation between two old women:

"For crying out loud, I says to him, let's get off the subject."

"And did he?"

"What do you think? Him get off a subject? He never gets off a subject. He jumps up and down on it till it's a patch of blood on the ground."

I drank another beer and felt a little drunk.

When I told myself, Maybe you're crazy, I heard, No, you're not, you're not crazy, you're something else.

I didn't call Henry.

13

———— • ————

I slept for a little while. I knew it was only a little while because I woke to the sounds of people in other rooms preparing to go to bed. I didn't sleep for the rest of the night.

In the morning, it was as if I had forgotten Henry, and nothing remained of his presence but my state of mind, which I didn't necessarily associate with him. With each day, perhaps, I would get further and further away from Henry until, in the end, I would wonder what state I was in. I couldn't now imagine the state would simply vanish with Henry's vanishing.

At the language school, while watching the talking mouth of a student, I wondered why people spoke.

As I watched a student write a sentence, I would wonder, why do people write?

As I went through the lessons, I found myself more and more impressed by my responsibility towards my students. I hated having to do what I did, but I did it, and I did it well. In that day's lessons I taught my Panamanian to speak, in the past, present, and future, and in the negative past, present and future. To do this I stood and took up positions that corresponded to different tenses and in each position I performed an act or did not perform an act: sleeping, eating, walking.

During lunch break, in a local cafeteria with another teacher from the school, I felt I didn't have the power to open my mouth to talk. Yet I did, and I admired myself, in some stark way, for what I would do whether I liked it or not. I imagined I had to move the hands of the clock on the wall to make the seconds of the afternoon class pass. But as I moved them with one hand, I taught with the other, and sometimes I moved them back to explain, once again, that in English you could not use a double negative. Sometimes I imagined I was trying to teach a language to natives, who had no language, to civilize them. The last hour took all my strength to move, at fractions of a second, the hands of the clock, and then the most difficult part of the day was filling out the class register.

Leaning back in my wooden chair, I asked myself: Where does this center of responsibility come from?

Before going to my room, I walked around the Public Garden, and there were long moments, filled with late sunlight, when I forgot I should be thinking about something. When I was reminded what I should be thinking about, it appeared not to bear much attention. I looked at people as though they were walking on the same paths as I was, as though they were in the same park as I was, as if they inhabited the space I inhabited.

I had walked among people on the streets, stood with them in lines at post offices and banks, sat with them in movie houses, without seeing them. My fantasy had been so strong, it could have limited my senses for my entire life, and I would never have recognized that I was limited by fantasy. It would have been very easy for me now to turn against that image, to turn against it and destroy it, rather than draw back from it and simply see it diminish in the outside air. I would have given up everything for even the faintest possibility of its being realized. I would have given up my friendship with Charlie and Roberta. And only I wouldn't have known that I'd given up everything for a banal image that was repeated again and again pornographically. How I hated fantasy. If there were no ways for my sex to enter into life, if my sex fixed me in fantasy, then I must give up my sex. I had enough control to do that.

As I was opening the door to my room, a large third-story room which overlooked a tree-lined alley, the telephone rang.

"Did you call him?" Roberta asked.

"I'm feeling better."

"You won't get over him unless you see him again."

"But I'm feeling better without seeing him."

"It's up to you – "

She put the responsibility on me, and she would be annoyed with me if I didn't fulfill it. I suspected that she wanted me to fulfill it for her sake, which meant she'd be even more annoyed with me if I didn't.

"Come on," she said, "show me you can do it."

"I can do it."

"Show me."

I asked to speak to Charlie, but she said he was out.

"Out where?" I asked.

"He went drinking with some friends from where he teaches."

"Oh," I said.

After I hung up, I looked at the telephone, and as I did I saw it flatten and become merely the image of a telephone. When I reached for the receiver, my hand and arm seemed to detach themselves from me and cease to have anything to do with me, and when I heard my voice say, "Hello," to a voice that said "Hello," it wasn't my voice, or his, I heard.

"It's Dan," I said.

I thought, Now you have risked everything.

After I hung up, I began to tremble. I told myself that my trembling, which made the desk chair creak, was exaggerated. When I tried to stop it, my arms and legs would break the self-restraint I was using, and jerk. Because I knew why I was trembling, I should be able to restrain it, but I couldn't. I yawned more and more as the trembling decreased.

I felt deeply sleepy.

I telephoned Roberta to tell her Henry and I would come round Saturday evening. She said, "Don't you feel better for doing it?"

"No," I said.

But I did.

For the rest of the week, I tried not to anticipate seeing him. Much as I told myself not to expect anything, I knew I expected everything. I would say out loud when I was alone, "You expect everything." But I did keep myself from anticipating what the

97

everything might be.

The only image that dramatized my anticipation came to me as I was standing at a corner waiting for traffic to pass: running. It surprised me that the image expressed my sense of accelerating longing for him. It surprised me and it pleased me. As I walked slowly, my mind ran and ran.

As it ran, I said, as if on a wild thrust forward, to run even faster, "I love him."

All day Saturday my mind ran faster and faster, and in the hour before I was to meet him it ran so fast I thought I wouldn't be able to stop and would burst past him.

He drove up, on time, in his car.

He must have just had a shower, as his hair was wet and his face shone. All at once he looked to me like a boy, not a man. Perhaps I looked the same. We were boys. But he had a man's voice.

"How do we get there?" he asked.

In the car beside him, I thought: I have spent half my life in this car.

Excited by being with him, and intimidated about expressing my excitement, I needed to contain it in some way, so I would contain it and express it in talking about our one permissible subject: books.

I translated his body into his talk about books. When we stopped at a red light and he unbuttoned two buttons on his shirt and ran his finger over the revealed skin, I thought: But my impression that he has no awareness of his sensual body must be wrong, he's very aware of it. In talking about literature, which was meant to de-personalize, he was being entirely personal; he wasn't rising above himself, but raising himself to the level of what he considered most important. I had imagined he was a person with a fine, transparent ego, but he might have had the biggest, most colored ego of anyone I'd ever met. Well, if he did, his ego was his right.

Listening to him, looking at him, I thought: No, you aren't wrong to be in love with him.

Climbing the wooden steps to the porch, I wished I was alone.

After I rang the doorbell and turned to see Henry in the yellow porch light, standing still with no expectations of any kind, I realized I wished I'd come alone because I wasn't sure Charlie and Roberta, who were in a way family to me, were people Henry would be interested to meet. He already knew he wouldn't be interested, and this was why he had no expectations.

I remembered when, in freshman year, I first took Charlie to visit my parents in our house, remembered my worry, as I opened the door into the entry, that our lives were nowhere near the level of his and his family. But Charlie being Charlie, said to my parents, "What a nice house you have." And, being me, I said, "Come on, I'll show you around." With each grim little room I showed him, he said, "This is pretty," and I'd say, "Isn't it?" We both knew what we were doing, and knew that this made us friends. With Henry (not that I wanted to compare him and Charlie) I would have had to say, The rooms are grim, and he would have, of course, agreed. This truthfulness, in a way, precluded our understanding one another and becoming friends. Charlie opened the door.

"Hello," he said, in a loud voice, holding out both hands and smiling.

I thought, How young we are.

Roberta did not make any special efforts with Henry, nor did he with her, but from the moment they met one another they talked, effortlessly, as they talked the whole evening.

He hardly spoke to Charlie, even during the moments he was alone with us when Roberta was in another room. Charlie tried at least to make Henry the center of the evening by saying, "What a pleasure it is to have someone visit for the first time," which Henry, stepping as it were to the side, smiled at a little.

I answered, "Yes."

Then Henry went off to find Roberta, into the bedroom to watch her, he said, take care of Jerry, or into the kitchen as she prepared supper.

I spent most of the evening with Charlie, both of us making efforts to talk to one another.

I said, "I think there's going to be another war."

He said, "Don't say that, Dan."

During the meal, Charlie said again and again, "This is great food, really great," followed immediately by my saying, "Really great." Henry didn't comment. Roberta said, "You two are very funny," then asked Henry, "Aren't they funny?"

He smiled again.

She said to him, "After dinner, they tap-dance on the table and sing."

"Are they good?" he asked.

She laughed. "They're terrible."

He laughed too. I hadn't seen him laugh. I'd thought he had no sense of humor. Charlie, too, was laughing at what Roberta said. I forced myself to.

I saw all the falsity of Charlie, and saw that we were similar. I was certainly more like him than Henry, which indicated, in its way, how little sex had to do with setting the terms of a relationship. I was not sexually attracted to Charlie, except at odd moments when I recalled how I had been, and I was again, for that moment, nostalgically attracted to him. And yet I was closer to him than to anyone else I knew. Roberta was right, we were a kind of comedy act, two loving bums who loved one another and whom no one else loved.

I resented Henry's lack of self-consciousness. His lack of falsity made him, I thought, less of a person. He was born into a state of self-possession. And this was why Charlie and I were not on his level. Charlie wasn't putting Henry at the center so that I would feel Henry was a friend of friends and not someone from the outside. Really, Charlie couldn't help putting Henry at the center. Our reasons for doing this were not dissimilar: if I wanted Henry at the center for his body, it was in his body that his self-possession most showed itself. Charlie and I sounded false in our honoring him, and we were false, because we did not know how else to be. Charlie, drunk, raised his wine glass to Henry and said, "To the hub of our evening," to which I, drunken and raising my glass, said, "To the hub of the hub," as if I were not going to allow Charlie to upstage me. But there was something more than the honor we showed the guest that Charlie and I shared, and we both knew it: our desire to make fun of Henry. We wanted to deride him for being at the center.

Roberta, also a Protestant, had what Henry had. But we didn't deride it in Roberta because she was a woman.

"Will you two ring down the curtain?" she said to Charlie and me.

But Charlie and I continued to talk to each other, assuming that what we said was important for the listening world.

"I do believe there'll be another war," I said.

"Don't," Charlie said.

"What do you mean, don't? Don't what? Don't say what's going to happen?"

"How do you know, Dan? How can you say you know?"

"I know," I insisted.

"You can't."

"I do."

Henry and Roberta talked about Boston.

I got drunk. I hoped Henry would, but he didn't. When I tried to fill his glass, he said, touching the rim with a finger to stop me, "I've got to drive." I refilled my glass. "I should be going," he said.

Charlie said to me, "If you're not going on to anywhere else, stay the night."

I didn't answer, but was angry at him, because I wanted to leave with Henry.

Staring straight at me, Roberta said, like a business woman, "It'd be better if you didn't stay. I've got a big day tomorrow, and – "

I hugged her.

Henry kissed her cheek and shook Charlie's hand with, I noted, a firm grip.

We were silent as he and I sauntered through the warm night to the car.

I was running, really.

He said, "If it isn't too personal, is Charlie the room-mate you were in love with?"

This shocked me. I said, "I don't mind your asking personal

101

questions," but my shock kept me from saying anything more.

"I'm sorry."

"But I don't mind."

"I wondered only because he is so beautiful."

"Charlie?"

"Yes."

"I guess I know him too well to see it."

"You can take my word for it."

After a moment, I said, "Yes, he is the person I told you about. But it didn't happen the way I said. That was fantasy. You must have known."

"I know it was a fantasy." We stood by the car. Henry asked, "What did happen?"

"Charlie and I have never mentioned it to one another."

I had Henry's interest and I wanted to keep it. "I'd like to say it was the most wonderful experience in our lives," I said.

"I'm sure you would."

I said, "It lasted about five drunken minutes, and I can hardly remember anything about it."

He asked, "And you're no longer attracted to him?"

"I am, at moments, but I don't think I could ever make love to Charlie, even if he wanted to."

"Why?"

"I know him too well."

He said, "I tell myself that the more I know a person the more I should want to make love with him."

I said, "But that's not the way it is."

"It should be."

Then he left me to go around the car and get in the driver's seat.

Driving, he said, "Roberta is interesting."

"She is."

Then he said, "She holds that family together."

I didn't know what he meant.

As he didn't say anything more about Charlie, I presumed he didn't find him interesting.

In my drunken state, I felt great sentimental love for Charlie.

I said, "Charlie's silly, but I love him. I love him for everything we've been through together. There've been some very silly moments."

I was about to go off on a long reminiscence of moments in Charlie's and my lives together in college, but I checked myself.

The silence in the car was Henry's, and it was intentional. He didn't want to speak. I wanted to speak, but didn't dare to, because he wouldn't answer. He was thinking, I imagined, about me, and I had no idea what he was thinking. Or maybe he wasn't at all thinking about me. I wondered how I could make him think about me if he wasn't.

Studying him as he drove, appearing in the sudden light of street lamps, then half disappearing, I imagined I had gotten to know him a little. Roberta was right to have thought that would happen. But she was wrong in thinking I would no longer want him, because I imagined, looking closely at him, that this happened: he, whom I was beginning to know as a person, had a body which existed apart from him, had a body which didn't essentially belong to him and could belong to me as well as to him. Solid as it was, it seemed to me that by reaching out for it with my arms I could remove it from him, and he, in some bodiless form, would continue to drive the car while I held his body against me, ready to jump out with it as soon as he stopped in front of my rooming house.

I wanted to steal his body. I should be able to do it. I thought, if I really put my mind to it, I should be able to get him to give it to me.

Somehow, it should be so easy, since neither of us really owned our bodies, to let them go off together, while I would sit with him and talk about whatever interested him: books. Our free bodies should be able to do what our bound bodies hadn't done when Henry last drove me home – go up to my room and make love. This seemed to me something neither of us could object to, and it would put right what had gone wrong. It was what our bodies instinctively wanted.

He knew he controlled his body and would only rarely give it the freedom it wanted. His free body would want to make love with mine. But he didn't want it to. I needed to break his control over it.

To say, as we were going down Marlborough Street, I'm not very tired, would have been a cheap way of letting him know that I wanted him to say, I'm not tired either. We weren't that cheap. Or at least he wasn't. I had only minutes, seconds, to think of something original that would inspire him to react to me, that would make him give over control to me. He could find anything I said cheap. What I needed to say was one sharp thing to convince him he should let his body go free. Only one sentence was needed. But it had to be a good one. If it wasn't, if it didn't convince him, I would risk everything and lose. He stopped in front of the rooming house and switched off the engine. I could have had him, I knew I could have had him, by saying the right thing. I could have said, Look, I love you and I want to make love with you, which was at that moment the most truthful thing for me to say. He raised his hand for mine. I couldn't take the risk. I held his warm hand only for a second before I got out of the car.

On the landing outside my door I stopped and placed against my face the hand he'd held.

14

———— • ————

I didn't sleep at all during the night, and at some point in the early morning I became aware, with a terrifying attention, of a function of my mind I'd never experienced before. Uncontrollably, my mind released image after image. I was not asleep. I was completely conscious and looking at a scene.

In my mind there appeared a square outside a train station at night, with hundreds of standing people, and soldiers brought a young man into their midst. The soldiers held the young man while doctors, in blood-stained smocks, undressed him, and the people around watched. One doctor looked down his throat, another grabbed his testicles and made him cough, another shouted at him to bend over and spread out his buttocks for a rectal examination. The doctors said, "All right," to the soldiers, who tied the naked young man to an electricity pole, and then the soldiers beat him with lengths of barbed wire. All the while the spectators were laughing. If I, studying the scene, wasn't laughing with them, I thought they were right to laugh at the young man for no other reason but that what he was going through was totally without originality, and therefore to be derided. It was as if the young man deserved what he was getting because he was, himself, unoriginal, and did not have the imagination to make up a more original dramatization of his thoughts and feelings. The jeering crowd had seen it all before, we all knew where.

Among the spectators, some people, turning away from the whipping, amused themselves by farting or seeing who could pee the farthest. I knew that if an equivalent had to be found between some image and what I thought and felt, it'd be among these people, not with the young man. They knew that what I was going through shouldn't be taken seriously. When, from among them, the image came to me of a naked, skinny man balancing on his head a naked, fat man, the one so skinny his cock was as big as a leg and the other so fat he hardly had a cock, I wondered if this was an equivalent: my state was as superficially silly, it really and truly was.

But the scene in the middle kept drawing me to it, as it became more and more violent. I did not want to look at it. This was not because I was upset by it, but because I was embarrassed by it. Perhaps the young man had staged it himself to demonstrate his state. Now, the soldiers were wrapping his body with the barbed wire, while he, dripping with blood, stood motionless, his eyes staring into the cavorting crowd. He wanted to be taken seriously, wanted the crowd to believe his feelings were equal to his pain, when all the crowd knew they weren't.

As I, in the crowd, looked at the young man, an old, toothless woman next to me said, hitting me in the side with her elbow, You feel bad for him.

I said to her, No, I don't.

Yes, you do.

I don't, I repeated.

An old man next to her said, I can see you do.

No, I insisted.

People around me laughed.

Then why aren't you having a good time, joking and laughing with us? the old woman asked.

All right, I said. I will. You'll all see: I'm the silliest person in the world.

He doesn't have it in him, someone said, to joke and laugh.

I do.

You're so serious.

I'm not.

You're so deep.

I'm not.

You have such deep and serious thoughts and feelings.

I don't. I don't.

A bearded transvestite pushed people aside and said to me, harshly, Then show us you can have a good time.

What do you want me to do?

He laughed.

I heard a groan. The soldiers were hefting the stiff, burnt carcass of a war victim onto the shoulders of the young man whose arms and legs were entwined with barbed wire. One soldier pushed him to start him walking. Nausea came over me for what I could only think was the sickening exaggeration of the scene; the very strain of the demonstration to be original belied the violence of it, made it dishonest. The people about me were honest; if they exaggerated, they did it deliberately, and had fun exaggerating. I kept looking at the young man, however, who staggered under the weight of the dead body as he walked towards the train station. I took a step in his direction.

In the crowd I heard a screeching laugh, and, startled, I turned to see, in the crowd but overlooking it, a horned monster, surrounded by the transvestite and the others who had derided me for having no sense of fun. The monster was looking at the young man make his way through the crowd, while the hot night sky was pulsing with the pink light of exploding bombs, and the monster's laughter rose higher than the bomb blasts. This, I knew, was the true metaphor for my state of being, this monster, for whom all metaphors were fake. It turned its head towards me a little and smiled at me with spiky lips, and I knew he knew the truth, knew that all things were vanity, so when, hearing a cry of pain from the young man, I looked round at him, I did so with the sudden terror that all he was suffering was vanity, that all the metaphors from my religion were vain. I hated that young man.

In the grainy, grey, dawn light, I got up from my bed, on which the sheets were twisted, and sat at my desk. I tried to write out, sentence after sentence, the most basic questions, thinking that in this way I was being reasonable, and what I needed to be above all was reasonable.

Be reasonable, I thought. Don't ask yourself, Why is this madness happening to me? because that will only bring you down to the level of the madness. Ask yourself simpler questions that have to do, not with what is happening to you, but with what you can do about it.

Ask yourself: What can you do to stop wanting what you can't have.

I wrote: I do not want to live with him. I do not want a friendship with him. I do not want –

I knew what I wanted, and there was nothing I could do to achieve it. No amount of the most reasonable thinking would realize that want or, by default, explain it away. Any attempt to explain it away brought me down again to the question Why do you want so much what you can't have? This, in turn, brought me down to other questions, each crazier than the last, so that I imagined it was my very attempt to ask reasonable questions, never mind answer them, that produced more fake monsters. They began to hang from the picture rail around the walls.

The room filled with hot sunlight.

When the telephone rang, I felt a moment of real fear.

Roberta asked me how I was.

"I'm all right."

"Are you sure?"

I said, "Look, I honestly don't want to talk about it."

"So it's not all right."

"Let's not exaggerate." I said, "It doesn't matter."

"It matters."

"It doesn't."

"Come over here," she said.

"I don't want to talk about it."

"Fine. We won't talk about it. But come over."

If I don't go, I thought, she'll be annoyed with me, and I can't allow her to be annoyed with me.

All my life, women made me do what I didn't want to do.

We sat in the backyard. Charlie held Jerry in his lap, and we talked for a while about his first tooth, which wasn't giving him any trouble.

Roberta said to me, "You don't want to talk about it, I know, but I wanted to tell you how much better looking than Henry you are. Charlie thought so too."

"You are," Charlie said. He was making an effort.

I laughed.

"I also happen to think you're more intelligent," Roberta said.

"Stop lying," I said.

"I mean it."

"It seemed to me he didn't have much to say," Charlie said.

"He had a lot to say," Roberta said, "but it was limited. He never talked about himself. I don't think he's had much experience to talk about. Did you know that he's never been abroad, for example?"

"No," I said.

"He's hardly ever left New England."

"I didn't know."

She said, "All he said to me that was interesting, I thought, was that at holiday dinners his family passed round genealogies, so relatives could try to figure out just how they were related to one another. That was the only personal thing he said. Otherwise, his talk was all commentary."

"I thought he was good at that," I said.

"Again, limited," she said. "Very limited."

I felt Roberta didn't have the right to be negative about Henry. She should have praised him, as he deserved. I didn't like what she was saying, and I didn't like the pleasure I was getting from it. Any reaction to Henry, whether negative or positive, was a false reaction.

I said, "Anyway – " as a way of changing the subject.

"I know, I know," she said, "you don't want to talk about him."

"Not really."

She said, "Now you should forget him and stop floating around, and get back to earth."

"What?"

She kept her eyes fixed on me, her smile, too, fixed. "You

know."

"I've never lost an hour's work," I said. "Ask Mrs. Hart, ask my students. I've been a good teacher all along."

She shook her head. "I didn't mean your teaching."

"What did you mean?"

Charlie was silent, trying to hold the baby, who punched him in the face and kicked his groin. It was as if he was trying to hold his worry about what was happening between Roberta and me.

"I wish you'd tell me," I said.

"You never want to talk about relationships."

I frowned.

"If you had really wanted a relationship with Henry, you could have tried to work for it. But it was obvious to me, when I saw you together, that you didn't. No doubt you're right, and he's not worthy of you. But I'm pretty sure he'd try to have a relationship with you if you'd only try one with him. I felt that about him, that he knows about family ties, and – "

I said, "I don't want a relationship with him."

"What else do you imagine happens when two people come together, even if for a fuck?"

"It's an experience you have to have had," I said.

"Don't you see that there is no basis, none at all, to loving someone except in a relationship, however complex, however massively complex, it is?"

I wished I could tell her how much I hated the way she spoke, the way she seemed to be trying to impress me with the way she spoke.

"I don't want to live with anyone," I said. "I can only think that to live with someone is to have a family, and I refuse to have a family."

"And friends?"

"And friends, if that means having to listen to them talk about my relationships with them and my responsibilities towards the relationships."

"Dan," Charlie said, bouncing Jerry up and down, "what else is there among people?"

"There's not having relationships," I said.

Roberta's voice rose. "There's taking from them but not giving anything to them."

I turned to her full face.

She said, "You're very good at imposing yourself on others and not good on letting others impose on you."

"I don't impose on others."

"Don't you? Don't you, didn't you, on Charlie?" She paused, and then she said, quickly, "Didn't you impose demands on Charlie that he had to accept, because he knew that otherwise you wouldn't keep him as a friend?"

Charlie got up and went into the house with Jerry.

Roberta said, "You want everything your own way, Dan. I admire you for that, I suppose, because so do I want everything my own way. And I'd no doubt admire you even more if you did get everything your way. But you won't."

I lowered my head and looked at my hands in my lap.

I wanted to say, For Christ's sake, tell a joke.

"The very quality in Charlie that keeps him your friend," she said, "is, I'm sure, the quality you least admire in him, if you've even suspected it in him. That's his sense of duty towards others. You think he's irresponsible, and you like it that he's irresponsible. But you've never noticed, I'll bet, how he tries not to be, and how he works to fulfill his duties. Your old irresponsible room-mate is working to realize his duties as a husband and father and as an art teacher and as an artist. If you considered, for a moment, your sense of duty towards him –" she stopped.

I intertwined my fingers.

She said, "He and I are trying to help you get over what's keeping you irresponsible. I'm not sure our help can do any good."

I squeezed my hands between my knees.

Leaning towards me, she said, "It's up to you," and she put her hands on my hands.

I asked, "Do you mind if I go home now?"

"Why do you think you need my permission?"

"I don't know," I stood. "I'll just go. I won't say goodbye to Charlie."

111

"He'll be offended."

"I'd offend him more, I think, if I saw him. Maybe I should stay away from Charlie."

"He'll be angry with me for having brought up what I did," Roberta said. "Maybe I shouldn't have."

"Say goodbye to him from me."

"Don't dramatize it too much. It's not as though you were never going to see one another again."

I smiled.

She said, "Listen, what I would do if I were you, which I know I'm not, would be to treat what you're going through as though it were a disease that has taken over your body. Like any disease, it has to be cured, and it can only be cured by people who know about curing."

"I could never make myself go."

She said nothing.

I said, "I'll go into the woods, and come out when I'm cured or I'll die in the woods."

"I wish you'd stay out of those woods," Roberta said.

I left by the gate between the house and the old garage.

The monsters in my room moved silently and swiftly when I wasn't looking; when I was looking, they remained still and invisible, and I knew that, though I could hardly see them, their presences were indicated by thin, horn- and spike-lipped smiles. They never stopped making fun of me. When I went into the bathroom to pee, I imagined they followed me in then followed me out, waddling on thick, squat, scaly legs, nudging one another, pointing at me, and stifling their laughter with wart-covered, knubbly-knuckled hands.

I wanted to turn to them and say, For Christ's sake, can't you be a little more original?

But that would have offended them, and I didn't want to offend them.

They jumped up and ran into the walls when the telephone rang.

Charlie said, "I'm sorry you left like that, without saying anything."

"It seemed the best thing to do at the time."

"I don't know, Dan. Roberta is a truthful person, and what she said she said because she believes the truth is best. She probably went too far, though."

"No," I said. "If anything, she didn't go far enough."

"Can't I see you?"

"I'm not in a very good state, Charlie."

"I know."

"You're the one who should be asking yourself if you want to see me."

"Come on," Charlie said. "We've seen one another through all kinds of strange times. Roberta's too pure, in a way. You've got to be very careful with Roberta. She doesn't understand that two people can have a relationship that's, well, odd according to certain ways of thinking, yet good. I try to tell her she has to take a more oblique view, but she can't. I know I can."

I said, "Let's leave it a while, and then we can get together and talk."

"I don't want to talk," Charlie said. "To tell you the truth, I think she's exaggerated it all. I mean, I don't believe that the way you think about me, or about Roberta either, has any connection with the way you think about this guy."

"Is that what Roberta believes?"

"I can't stand her talking about it any more. She's out now. I told her to go away to visit a friend for a couple of hours. It's become too much."

"I don't understand."

"Neither do I. Roberta's desire to get things right makes her a great person, in a way, but – "

"She wants to get me right?"

"I'll tell you, Dan, that sometimes I get tired listening to her talk on and on about you."

Without saying anything, I delicately lowered the receiver. Then I pressed my nose against a white piece of paper, my eyes staring at it. The telephone rang again. It continued to ring, and wouldn't stop until I answered.

"Dan," Charlie said.

"I'll speak to you some time next week," I said.

"I'll get in touch with you if you don't with me."

"I'll get in touch," I said.

"I wish you hadn't hung up on me," he said.

"I'm sorry."

I didn't want Charlie to see me. He should think I was incapable of being unhealthy. I needed to be, to him, perfect.

Then I thought, It is just because you feel this that you should see him, should let him see you.

I had, I'd thought, hidden so much from Charlie. I had hidden all my sins. Or I had tried to.

The sun was still up when I went to the bar, not the bar near the bus station I usually went to. It was dark inside. There I picked up a young man named Karl. The sun had set by the time we left the bar to go, first for something to eat, then to his place. We could walk there, he said. We went into the South End, to a street where all along the sidewalks and gutters were shattered liquor bottles thrown by derelicts from the windows of their rooms. Not even the poor lived in this neighborhood, just derelicts and gypsies and Karl. His room was above an old shop inhabited by gypsies. As we climbed, he told me to be careful of the bottles on the stairs. He didn't apologize. I had the feeling that I had been here before, or, at least, that it was as I had expected. Karl talked non-stop. He, too, seemed familiar to me.

He was young, maybe seventeen. He was effeminate.

I was sure I had heard everything he told me before. He didn't know who his father was and, since leaving his mother a couple of years before, he hadn't seen her. When he stopped going to school at sixteen, he started working. His job was in the kitchen of a hotel restaurant. He lived alone, and he'd done up his room.

Opening the door, he stood to the side to let me go in first. The light was on, and I saw a big brass bed in a small room. On the bed was a royal blue, chenille-like spread, with royal blue bolsters and throw pillows in what looked like pale blue satin cases, and everything was fringed. The draperies on the windows were royal blue, too, and hung in deep velvet folds from beneath a velvet valance, all, again, fringed in gold. The room was painted pale blue. The light, refracted, came from a small chandelier hanging from a cracked but painted ceiling.

Karl stood beside me. I presumed he thought I was so surprised I couldn't speak. He put a hand on my shoulder.

"I saved and saved for the fucking bed," he said. "Then when I got that together I saved for all the materials, and I made all the fucking drapes and the bedspread and everything."

"It's a beautiful room," I said.

"I worked hard enough for it."

"You should be an interior decorator."

"I do it for myself."

Looking around more, I said, "But where do you keep your clothes and things?"

"I put them in boxes under the bed," he said.

In this room, I thought, I won't be able to make love with Karl. His effeminacy had put me off him from when we'd started to talk in the bar. This was because I always felt effeminates were affecting their effeminacy; I found myself wanting to say to them, "Stop acting." This room gave the act its setting. I could not, ever, make love without feeling at some level in the love making that my life depended on it. There was no way life could depend on Karl in his room. I wondered how I could leave without hurting him. As much as I could have hated Karl for being so fake, however, I made myself take his hand from my shoulder and kiss it.

"Wait, wait," he said, and stepped away to pull from under the bed a cardboard box from which he took a negligee. "Turn away," he said, raising a commanding hand. When he commanded, "Now look," I turned back to see him in the negligee. With a hand on a hip, the other at the back of his head, he thrust one knee forward on the edge of the bed so the gown was held parted to reveal his cock and balls.

No, I thought, I can't.

I wanted to get away from him, I realized, not because he was pretending to be a woman, but because he in no way equivocated about it. He wasn't being ironical about his negligee or his room. It didn't occur to him that I might not find the act as wonderful as he did. It did not even occur to him that it was an act.

If I had sensed in him the slightest sadness, I might perhaps have felt sympathy for him. But there was no sadness in him. He was all brightness. He flashed around the bed, swinging the negligee open as he strode to reveal his long, white, slender, and beautiful body. I couldn't stand his spirit. He threw off the gown and, naked, came to me and put his arms around me.

I made myself make love with him with great and delicate affection. I wanted him to believe in my affection. In the rumpled bed, he himself rumpled, his hair messed and pungent smells penetrating his cologne, a moment came when, suddenly apart from him and looking at him, I saw that he was helpless, and the sense of his helplessness was all that was needed for me to make love with him as if his life depended on it. He was startled enough by my intensity to give in to it, and I found myself crouching on the bed with him in my arms, keening and kissing his face. I felt his body stiffen, and I let him go. I turned away from him.

A moment later I asked him where the toilet was.

He didn't know what had happened, but he knew I was using the toilet as an excuse to get away.

"It's on the landing. Put your shoes on, or you'll be crushing roaches with your feet."

When I got back, he looked at me as if expecting me to say I had to go.

"Can I ask you something?" he said.

"What?"

"You're not falling in love with me or anything like that, are you?"

"Why do you want to know?" I asked.

"Because I've got to tell you I'm not dependable." He tickled me under the arm, and as if he had touched the most senstive spot on me, my body jolted and I began to laugh. He kept tickling. "You're not, are you?"

"Stop it," I shouted.

He held me tightly and continued to tickle me while I writhed with laughter.

"Stop it, stop it."

"Tell me you don't love me."

I howled with laughter. It was as loud as unrestrained screaming. He was strong, and held me tightly while he hardly touched the tips of his fingers to my side.

Gasping, I shouted, "I don't love you."

15

———— • ————

Though I was not able to sleep in my bed, I felt, each morning, that I wouldn't be able to get out of my bed. I lay and watched the clock on the bedside table, thinking, It'll go past the time when I must get up, and then it will be too late, and then, when it is too late, there will be nothing I can do, so I'll stay in bed. But I did get up in time and went to work.

I saw no one outside the language school.

My Panamanian student, towards whom my feelings were becoming more and more loving the less he was able to learn, brought me this composition:

About of Boquete
In this composition, I have to like in narrate about of a small town from Panama. Boquete is situate on a Volcano.
The End

José was missing his country very much, and as I asked him questions, tears rose to his eyes. Tears then rose to my eyes.

At those moments when I thought I would not be able to do anything, I found myself longing for Henry as if he were an age in which a culture had realized its highest ideals. And now what was left of that civilization was broken statues.

Charlie knocked on my door. He had a bottle of whiskey, which he put on the floor of my room. For a moment, I felt my sinuses begin to fill with tears. But when he stood with his arms out and said, "Let's forget about our responsibilities and have a good time," a rage went through me and burned the tears. It was as if the rage had been in me since the first time I'd seen Charlie, just seen him, when he came into the dormitory room where I was sitting on my assigned bed and wondering who my room-mate would be. He had startled me, clapping his hands and saying, "We're going to have a good time in this room." He gave me now the same smile he gave me then.

I had never been able to get Charlie to admit, not even for a moment, that anything was wrong. In our years as room-mates, some students asked me how I could stand him, he was so irresponsible, but for Charlie everything was fine. And I went along with him, and was even proud of him for insisting that everything was fine. After he did body exercises in our room that kept me from studying, he would say, sweating and leaning over my desk, "Isn't it great being room-mates?" and I would suppress my irritation, thinking his activity was more important than my stillness. Really, I should have been as positive as he was. When I'd gone out with him on dances, I'd tried to be like him, but I resented having to be. I resented him telling me what a good time I'd have, was having, had had. Now, it came to me as never before that he must see there was no way I was going to raise myself and have a good time with him, and I felt in my rage the strength to pull him down with me. We were not going to have a good time. It was exactly about responsibilities that I wanted to talk with him.

I turned away from Charlie and said flatly, "The only good time I can have is dead."

"Come on, Dan," he said.

I turned back to him. I knew that what Charlie found most unbearable was, as he would have said, locking feelings into grand gestures and grand words. His enthusiasms were demonstrated by a lilt in his voice and a clap on the shoulder, and no more. He was pretentious, but his pretentions were, really, modest, as if he thought he could get away with them. He would not allow himself the great pretentions, the great negations. These expressions more than embarrassed him, they frightened him. I wanted to frighten him.

I stared at him and, keeping my voice low, said, "You'd better get out of here before I knock you down, too."

He picked up the bottle and held it towards me. "Come on."

"I'm not going to get drunk."

Twisting off the cap, he said, "I will," and he took a gulp. He sat on the edge of the bed with the bottle between his knees.

I sat at my desk, the chair turned to half face him.

"Roberta sends her love," he said.

"Does she? I thought she finally recognized last time I saw her that I'm too low to be loved."

Charlie laughed and held out the bottle. "I'm not going to leave before you take that back, because you know it's not true."

Leaning far over, I took up the bottle, gulped from it, and held on to it by the neck. Wincing, I stared at Charlie. "You have never known what is true about me."

He reached for the bottle. "Come on, Dan," he said. But I remained motionless and Charlie lowered his arm.

"Give me the bottle, Dan," he said.

After another gulp from it, I gave him the bottle.

I said, "You'll be sorry you're making me drink."

Charlie laughed, but it was a forced laugh. I could see the crooked hairs of my brows above my narrowed eyes. Charlie put the bottle on the floor between us.

I said, "At the same time, I think you do know what's true about me, have known it for years, and you've never been able to admit it."

He laughed again. "Never been able to? I could have admitted it if I'd wanted, but I never wanted to."

I sat back in my chair.

"Let's forget this," Charlie said. "Let's just get drunk together."

I said, "No, I'm not going to forget it."

Charlie picked up the bottle and handed it to me. I stood, drank from it, handed it back to him, and walked up and down the side of the bed where he sat. I stopped in front of him.

"Admit it, then, admit it now."

"Dan – "

"Admit it."

"I was joking."

"You weren't joking."

"You know I'm always joking."

"Admit it."

"Dan, please, I came here to make up for last time. Maybe it was my fault, what happened, as much as Roberta's. I thought Roberta was forcing something, to tell you the truth, as I was – "

"You know it was my fault. You've come with a bottle of whiskey and a generous heart to forgive me my sins, though, in your generosity, you wouldn't want me to think you thought I'd sinned against you, you'd generously want me to think you'd sinned against me. You're so nice, Charlie."

"Dan, don't say anything you'll be sorry for. Once you put your feelings into words, you'll regret them. Don't – "

"I'll say anything I want." I flung up my arms. "I'll do anything I want."

"Dan – "

"The fact is, you want me drunk because you want to hear me say what I want. You like me to do what you can't do, make grand pronouncements, make grand gestures. You can't say what you want, ever. I know you. You want to know what I think about you, what I really think, that you hope I can only admit with the grandest words and gestures." I spread my legs and stretched out my arms wide, and I lifted my head. "Oh, you're so nice, Charlie."

He stood. His closeness to me surprised us both, and we stepped away from one another.

I said, "That's the grandest pronouncement I have to make about you: you're so nice."

"I'm not," he answered.

"You are."

In a low voice, he said, "I'd like you to think I am, I've always wanted you to think I am, but I'm not."

"I know you. You're such a clean cut, all American boy, you help old women and dogs, you say hello to the mailman, you can't think an unkind thought about your neighbor. You wouldn't even turn against someone who was trying to kill you, as I – "

"Dan, you don't know – "

"You don't have it in you to be bad."

He shut himself up, as though he didn't want to say what he was thinking. He drew in his chin and his neck bulged his collar. His eyes were large.

"I'm the bad one," I said, "and you know it. Admit it. Go ahead, admit it. You like being with me to see how un-nice a person can be, to hear someone else say everything you'd never allow yourself to say, because you know that what I'm saying is what you believe and would never admit you believe. You have a responsibility to tell the truth. Friends have a responsibility to tell the truth about their relationships."

Charlie said quietly, "Dan."

"The real reason why you came to see me," I said, "was because you wanted to see how un-nice I am."

His voice went high, like a woman's. "If you continue like this, I'll go. I don't want to leave you in a state like this. But I will."

"Go."

He turned round, as if searching for something, then he sat back on the bed.

I said, "Now admit to me what you've always hated about me."

Looking up at me, he licked his lips.

I leaned over him. "Admit it." I took the bottle from between his knees where he held it, drank, and gave it back to him. I said, "Tell me."

"I've always loved you."

"Tell me what, for years and years, you've found so unbearable about me you've wished I'd die from it."

His eyes, raised to mine, opened so all the blue irises showed.

"Tell me," I said.

"You wouldn't want to hear."

"Come on, come on," I said, "I can already see it in your eyes."

The muscles of his face tightened.

122

"In all the years of demands I've made on you," I said, "demands for more, much more, always more, than you wanted to give, you had to have had bad thoughts about me. When, at the lake, I – "

But I stopped when I saw Charlie's eyes focus now with anger. We had never mentioned what had happened between us at the lake perhaps because to bring it up was embarrassing. It gave significance to what now had little significance, and this, I knew, angered Charlie.

He said, "I hated, and hate, your jealousy."

I stood back.

"You're jealous of me, of me and Roberta, of me and Roberta and Jerry."

"Jealous," I said.

"You were when we were room-mates. You couldn't stand me talking in the shower with some of the guys while you were in our room. You were jealous of me and the guys. You were jealous of the entire college. There were times when I thought you were jealous of the whole city of Boston. There were times when I thought you were jealous of America."

I looked at the floor. After a while, I turned round to my desk and sat at it and looked at a piece of paper.

He got up from the bed and came to the desk, but stood behind me. "Let's not go on."

I looked at him over my sholder. He smiled and held out the bottle. I took it, drank, and handed it back. I was drunk. I stared again at the piece of paper on my desk while Charlie stood behind me.

I said, "Jealousy is the one notion I know I am sincere about."

In his silence, Charlie didn't deny this.

The telephone rang.

Turning to Charlie, I said, "That must be Roberta checking to find out if I've killed you."

"She wouldn't do that."

"You answer."

He picked up the telephone receiver, said, "Well hi, how are you? Yes, fine, really fine," and held out the receiver to me and said, "It's your friend Henry."

16

———— • ————

Henry's voice sounded thin over the telephone. He asked, "How's your work going?"

As I didn't know what he meant by my work, I answered, "All right. And yours?"

"I keep at it," he said.

"That's good."

He said, "I thought I'd take a break. I've been invited to a party tonight. I was told to take anyone I wanted, so I thought I'd ask you if you'd like to come."

I almost said, No, I can't tonight.

The nerves of my body seemed to expand suddenly so I felt myself become enormous, and out of control.

"I'd like to come."

After I hung up, that sense of an expanded self, with only the most delicate points of control within it, stayed with me. I was so little in control, Charlie could have said to me, You can't go to the party, and I would have submitted. I would have, in an almost completely detached way, done anything Charlie asked of me, but I waited for him, and wanted him, to tell me I must go.

Charlie said, "Do you want me to go home?"

"I won't be leaving till later. But I don't think you'll want to wait."

"Not really."

For a long while after he left, I felt lost, and walking around my room I bumped into furniture on my way to I was never quite sure where.

It was not the anticipation of seeing Henry that caused this effect on me, I realized, but my letting Charlie go.

Bumping into a door jamb, I thought, What have I done?

As I changed my clothes I considered carefully what I would wear, then decided I mustn't do this, and put back on the clothes I'd taken off.

I was thinking, What have I done to Charlie? while going downstairs to meet Henry.

I saw him standing by the car and I thought, I love him, as if the thought occurred for the first time, not in my mind, but in my body, and it gave to the body its impulse to make a great gesture. It was in me to make such gestures, and as I walked down the steps to him I imagined I was, inside, throwing myself from the last step to lie on the sidewalk before him. It was only when I felt my knees and elbows and my chin strike the cement that I knew I had given in to the impulse. The blood I tasted rising between my teeth was still more imaginary than real, but it was real enough for me to suck it back and swallow it. I reached for his legs and half wailed, "Ah." He quickly leaned over to put his hands under my arms to raise me, and when I was on my knees, he, too, got down on his knees to support me.

"Are you all right?" he asked again and again.

For a moment I leaned all my weight on him, and he was forced backwards trying to keep me up. My cheek pressed his. He drew his head further back to see me.

"Are you all right?"

I looked into his eyes and I felt that I made another wild gesture with my arms and legs and torso, all projected out through my eyes. His eyes went blank.

Pulling away from him, I said, "I'm all right."

"Are you sure?"

"Yes." I got to my feet. "I slipped."

He stood, too, but kept a hand on me to steady me.

Examining my trousers at the knees and my shirt at the elbows, I said, "They're not even torn."

He let me go and frowned.

125

"Honestly," I said, "I'm all right."

At the party I knew no one, and Henry didn't introduce me to anyone, not even the host. He stood with me to the side of a large room, half turned away from the crowd of men, and he talked to me. I kept telling myself that I should have been pleased that I was the only one he was attentive to, but I also told myself I was bored by Henry's talk, which was about what he'd been reading. I was pleased that he took me to be up to his talk, saying from time to time, "You'd understand this," but I wondered why he had come to a party to stand so at the edge of it that he was hardly there, and to talk about what had nothing to do with the party.

You would have had a better time if you'd stayed with Charlie, I heard myself say.

And yet Henry was standing next to me within reach. It didn't matter what he said as long as he was standing next to me. He was concerned about me and had decided to stay with me all evening. I stared at his lips as he spoke, and I wondered what he would do if, as I had an urge to do, I kissed him. I couldn't believe he hadn't kissed with those lips and made love with that body over and over again, simply because to do anything else but kiss and make love would have been a waste, would have been to deny the lips and body their nature. What a waste, I thought, what a waste. And then it came over me that Henry's sex did not tolerate his being kissed by, his making love with, men.

As though the awareness had come to him by some extra-visual sense, I saw him, with a quick shift of his eyes to their corners, glance at a young man standing alone and facing the room. I looked at the young man, long enough for Henry to see that I was, and when I looked back at Henry I smiled. He didn't smile.

Standing side by side, I felt I could talk with no sense of consequence, as if we were, say, room-mates at a college dance only interested in one another enough to talk for a while, however intimately, because there was no one else to talk to. For the moment, we could think of nothing to say to one another, and I asked:

"Have you ever had a close relationship with anyone?"

When I spoke, I realized that this was the most important talk we could have.

He said, "I've tried."

"I wonder if that's something you can't try for, but something that has to happen of itself."

"I think it has to be worked on."

"I see."

He looked over my head. "Though maybe you're right and I'm wrong. I like things to happen rather than make them happen."

Rising a little on my toes, I tried to look him in the eyes. I said, "I thought you were like that because of me."

He lowered his eyes to mine. "Why you?"

"Because you've got to be careful with me in case I interpret something you say or do to mean something it doesn't. I'm always interpreting what you say and do."

"Why should you do that?"

He looked over my head again. I left him to go to another part of the room to look for the young man. I couldn't find him, and looked back to see Henry, standing, as if by choice, on his own among people talking to one another. He seemed to be looking to the side at a wall. He put his hands to his face. I thought I was seeing him at a moment of desperation. I went back to him quickly. I wanted to get to him before he lowered his hands, as if what I had been shocked into doing was to help him at this moment. He lowered his hands. His face was set.

I said, "Do you want to go?"

Frowning a little, he said, "Go where?"

Perhaps, I'd seen the desperation in him because I wanted to see it. His set face was calm.

I stood silently beside him and we looked at the people about us.

With a little jerk towards him, I asked, "What moment with someone else do you most remember?"

He stared at me. Quietly, he said, "I was just thinking about that."

127

My pulse began to beat in my neck. "Were you?"

He continued to stare at me. "I was walking through woods in New Hampshire with a friend. He was playing a harmonica. That was all."

We could have gone on talking, I felt, in the way we were, both a little sad because of circumstances that had nothing to do with one another but which brought us close.

It seemed to me that he had, walking through the woods with his friend playing the harmonica, done more, with more passion, than I could ever do.

I remembered that at the hops I used to go to with Charlie I talked and talked to girls while the band played and others danced. Then, suddenly in a pause, the thought apparently not having come to me before, because our talk was so interesting and neither she nor I would really have wanted to do anything but stand and talk, I asked, "Oh, would you like to dance?" It was only in retrospect that you realized the girl was longing to dance. Now that I had grown up enough to deal with hops, I had no idea if the man next to me wanted to dance with me. Henry, for all his uncompromising sexuality, might repulse any man who got too close to him. And yet I said to him, "Wouldn't you like to dance?"

He smiled and said, "No, thanks."

I had taken a very weak drink, but even so my mind swung out. I told myself I mustn't drink more. My mind would swing very far, yanking me out with it, and, if it let me go, I had no idea what I would do.

A voice said, Let go.

No.

What I did next, I did with what I believed was total control. I thought, All right then, if this is the way I am, I'm going to act out of unforgivable, unrepentant jealousy. It gave me the control to say to Henry, "Then I'm going to go find someone to dance with."

He blinked.

"Do you mind?"

"No, of course not."

I went, to let him know what I could do, to the young man who was now on the other side of the room. His name was Tom. He must have been eighteen or nineteen. Talking a little to one another, I held him loosely in my arms. Then, with a sense of complete control, a control that seemed new to me, I brought the boy to Henry to introduce him. Henry shook his hand.

I said to Henry, "Wouldn't you like to dance with Tom?"

Henry drew his chin in as his eyes widened. It pleased me that he was angry. He couldn't have been angry enough with me.

"Wouldn't you both like drinks?" Henry asked.

"That's good of you," I said.

Henry left and I stood in silence with Tom, to whom I was not attracted. I thought Henry wouldn't come back. When he did, with one drink in one hand and two in the other, I felt my control deepen. He gave a glass to Tom, then one to me, and raised his own halfway between the boy and me before he drank.

He asked Tom, "Are you a student?"

"I'm a college sophomore."

"What are you studying?"

While Henry asked Tom questions which he answered in a disconnected way, I ran my finger round Tom's neck, under his collar, and drank with the other hand. I imagined Henry didn't like, and wouldn't allow himself, these intimacies between men.

You shouldn't be drinking, I told myself.

Henry drank quickly. He went for another, saying he'd be right back. Tom said he wanted to dance again; as much as I didn't want to, we put our glasses on a table and our arms around one another and we danced where we were. I didn't want Henry to come back and not see us holding one another.

Tom asked, "Are you lovers?"

"Henry?"

"I wondered. You look as if you are."

I said, "He's not my lover."

"Then I can say I don't like him," Tom said.

"Why?"

"He has to be as cold in bed as he is out."

"Cold?"

"Isn't he?"

"No," I answered.

I wanted to go to Henry and say, I understand, I know what you feel, and that admission, said with passionate commiseration for what I knew he endured, would have us weeping in one another's arms.

I pressed my nose, my brow, into Tom's cheek, and I felt my tears stream down between our faces. I hoped he would think it was sweat. He didn't. He pulled his head back and looked at me.

"What's wrong?"

"I shouldn't be drinking," I said.

You're losing control, I said to myself, you really are losing control.

I broke away from him and went to Henry.

"Do you want to go home?" I asked.

"Home?"

"I mean," I said, "do you want him?"

"I don't want him if you do."

"If he doesn't want you, I don't want him either." I was wiping my eyes with my palms.

"I don't know what you mean," he said.

He knew.

I said, "I can't ever think of you as being capable of doing anything silly. Maybe I should leave before I do."

"Silly?"

"Before I take home with me the boy you want."

Henry said, "That wouldn't be silly."

His arms akimbo, Tom was waiting for me. I held him around the waist with an arm and drank as we revolved. The more we revolved, the more he laughed. I didn't laugh.

What I will show Henry, I thought, is that I can let go. I will show him that I do, always do, what I want. If I wanted to let go, no one would stop me. All that mattered to me now was that he should be watching me.

I was going to do something I had never done before, and I didn't know what was going to be revealed to me when I did it. I took Tom's glass from him and put it, with mine, on a table, and

130

as we continued to revolve, now in the center of the room, so people had to move out of the way, I began to unbutton his shirt, and he, laughing, unbuckled my belt. We lurched a lot as we undressed one another in a space now made into a circle by people watching. What was revealed to me was this: that my self-consciousness, at what should have been its apogee, left me. As Tom pulled my trousers down, I stepped out of them, then stepped out of the underpants he pulled down. I held up a foot for him to pull off my sock, and almost fell backwards, which had the crowd around us shouting, but I knew that the most embarrassing act I could commit among them would not embarrass me. And what I was doing concerned me as little as our being watched. My only point of reference was Henry. I didn't care if he hated what I was doing. Maybe I even wanted him to hate it. Tom stood, the hand with sperm covered fingers held out, as if to give it to someone. He smeared it over my chest and stomach.

Henry had left. Not even collecting our clothes and dressing made me feel anything except that I'd done something I wanted to do. I had made Henry go. A man, who turned out to be the host, came toward Tom and me carrying two fizzing high-ball glasses which he gave to us, then, slapping us on our backs, he said, "You're all right, you're really all right." I drank, thinking there was nothing else I would do if I got drunker. While I talked to the host, Tom walked away.

17

———— • ————

Henry had seen my sins. There was no way I could wipe out those sins, because there was no way I could make him not see them. If my sins were those that my romantic agony aspired to – the great sins – I would perhaps have been proud of Henry's seeing them in me. But, instead, they were the sins for which there was no forgiveness because they were not important, not even interesting, enough to be forgiven. What had happened was that Henry had seen my sins and ceased to be interested in me. I had done nothing by my act of jealousy but bring on Henry's condemnation. For two days, then another, I lived under the condemnation.

There were moments when I enjoyed this feeling of unworthiness.

When, kneeling for a long while in the center of my room, my arms hanging by my sides, my head bent, swaying a little, I felt that I was about to be justly punished for being an incompetent, a kind of shocked awareness of my humiliating submission made me get to my feet quickly. I told myself I must never, ever, do that again.

And yet I wanted to live on risk. My life should be made up of risks, one after another, leading me further and further into what I could not imagine, and wanted to imagine.

The greatest risks for me were not the risks of madness or suicide – I knew I was nowhere near going crazy or killing myself, however much I may have fantasized about these – but of pretension and self-indulgence. I knew I must risk these in loving, because without them I couldn't love.

I knew that the greatest risk I had to take was to call Henry and ask him to let me see him. I did not enjoy the humiliation I felt in dialing his number at work. His voice was cold. I tried to keep any supplication out of my own voice.

"I'll meet you anywhere you want. I'll meet you at the library if you'd like, and go along with you on your way home so I won't take up any of your time."

He said, "You'd better come to my home, about 10:30."

"I'll stay only fifteen minutes."

I could make myself telephone Henry, but I couldn't make myself telephone Charlie.

As I walked across the Public Garden, I felt better, and as I was climbing Beacon Hill, I felt so much better I thought that I didn't need to be going to see Henry, that, even without seeing him, I would have got over my love for him.

Following him into his small living room, I thought: The only risk I was taking was of being foolish, and that would be much less foolish than he had already observed me to be. In the hot room he was sweating. Sweating too, I said, "I want to tell you, as a simple statement, that I love you."

He said, "I should have told you when I met you that I was just getting over a bad relationship with someone who used to live here with me. It's weak of me, but I couldn't take on another relationship. There's nothing I admire more than close relationships, but I don't feel I'm up to one."

I sat on the edge of the sofa. "You don't understand. I don't want a close relationship with you. I don't even want to see you." I said, "I've become possessed by an idea of you that I think doesn't have anything to do with you." I put a hand to my head. "And yet, I think it must have everything to do with you."

He said, "I'm sure it doesn't have anything to do with me."

"Don't say that."

"You don't know me, so how can it have anything to do with me?"

"It sometimes seems to me that in carrying around the notion of this most beautiful person – you – I'm carrying around the most perfect and lucid idea a man can have. My mind is a closed room containing this amazing picture. But what should be wonderful isn't. I don't know why it isn't, but it isn't. It's horrible." I dropped my hands.

Wincing a little, he said, "I'll help you break it."

I said, "I don't want that." I got up.

"I can do it."

"I should go. I've been here longer than I said I would."

"You can stay."

When he put his hand on my arm, as if to hold me back, I pulled away. I left quickly.

My students frowned at me when I tried to explain simple points of grammar. Maybe, I thought, I wasn't saying what I thought I was.

Mrs. Hart told me I should go away for the weekend.

Instead, I called Charlie and went to see him and Roberta. None of us mentioned Henry. I studied them to make out the terms of their relationship.

18

———— • ————

I went to different bars in Boston, and one night met Tom O'Neill, who came back to my room with me. In the midst of our love making, I felt my chest seem to expand out towards him with love so sudden it surprised me. I didn't want to feel such love for anyone but Henry, and I tried to hold it in, but it went out to this young man, as if it were reaching out, with a little muscular spasm, for almost anyone. I didn't understand. Tom was in fact more beautiful then Henry. But his naked body appeared to me a pretence, and as a pretence it was ugly. The very shape of the body struck me as ugly, and I wondered how people could be attracted to one another for their bodies. I pretended to fall asleep. He fell asleep before me.

Sunday, we went to the Museum of Fine Arts. He was not interested, however, not even in the statue of the nude torso of the boy I took him to see. Later, we walked through the Fens, looking, as he said he liked to do, at people.

During the weekday evenings, I read novels. I had told my Panamanian student he should read books to improve his English. "What books?" he asked. "Try novels," I said. He looked at me with an expression of high disapproval and answered, "On, no, not novels." To him, novels, if not exactly immoral, did not add to one's moral vision and were a waste of time. For me, to read a novel was to improve one's moral vision, but this attitude was, I realized, unfounded. Novels added, perhaps, to one's understanding, but not to one's faith. José struggled through a few of the *Lives of the Saints*, which he said he had found in a Catholic bookshop. His English, after all my work, was no better at the end of the summer, when he returned to Boquete. I read many novels.

With Tom, on Friday and Saturday nights, I went to movies or to restaurants, then we separated for the night. If he telephoned at the last minute to break a date, I didn't mind. I thought I should start a friendship with Tom which would be based on an understanding that we were free, and that we would come together only at those points on which we agreed. Our relationship would be open to all possibilities because it would be open to everything around us, for no symbolic system would be imposed on it and reduce it to responsibilities towards one another. It seemed to me that two men did not have duties towards one another.

Roberta came to see me. It was as if Henry had never occurred in our relationship. She lay by me on my bed, each of us propped up by a pillow, and we ate sandwiches and drank frappes. She stayed on and on, until she finally said, "Charlie will think I've left him." Then she said, "He gives me reason enough to want to."

I didn't wish to talk about Charlie, but I said, "I can't imagine Charlie doing anything that'd make anyone want to leave him."

"You don't know Charlie."

"Yes, I do."

"Charlie would never show you, or any man, sides of himself that he shows me." After a silence, she said, "But let's not talk about Charlie. Let's not talk about relationships. We were having such an interesting conversation before."

"Yes," I said.

"Anyway, you never want to talk about relationships. To get you to talk of your thoughts and feelings about others is like trying to get Jerry to talk."

After she left, her smell remained about the bed, and on the pillow were strands of her blond hair. I thought I would be able to sleep.

One weekend morning while I was cleaning my room, Roberta telephoned and, in a high voice, asked if she could come see me right away. I was a little worried that she was coming to see me too often. Though I was going to stay in, I wanted to keep my day free, as I wanted, I told myself, to keep my life free.

As I was closing the door behind her, she said, "I've got to leave Charlie. I've got to." She sat at my desk and I on the edge of my bed. A hand raised to her temple, she said, "I can take his irresponsibilities. In a way, I'm even amused by them, but I can't take his fits – "

"Fits?" I asked.

"You don't know? You've never seen Charlie angry?"

"No."

"That's not possible."

"I never have."

She said, "Just last night, he threatened to burn the house down."

"Charlie?"

"I ran out of the house with Jerry, got into the car and drove to Charlie's parents' house and spent the night there."

I stood.

Roberta said, "I'm not sure whether I have a house to go back to, or a pile of charred ruins."

"I don't understand," I said.

"No?"

"Will you call him," Roberta asked, "just to find out if the house is still there?"

She got up from the desk chair to let me sit before the telephone.

Charlie's "Hello" was sullen, but when he heard my voice his changed, and he said, "Hey, hi."

I told him I was getting in touch just to find out how everyone was and I hoped I'd see him soon.

"What about tonight?" he asked. "What about going out and doing something together?"

I couldn't, I said; I had a stack of students' essays to correct.

"You sound all right," he said.

I was, I answered.

"It's always great to hear from you," he said.

137

"And Roberta and Jerry are well?" I asked.

"Very well," he said with a lilt. "We're all very well."

I hung up.

Roberta was leaning a thigh against the desk. "What do you think?" she asked. "Should I go back to him or not?"

"How can I say?"

She thrust herself away from the desk and walked about the large room. "Every possible reason is against it." As she continued to walk about the room, I watched her. Her hair, in one long blond braid at her nape, was pulled back from her finely angled face. "Tell me what we should do," she said to me.

"I'm not sure I can."

"You have so much influence over Charlie." She stopped in front of me. "You have so much influence over me."

"I do?"

"Over us both," she said. "You won't talk about relationships, I know. That's not what I mean. I mean being with you makes a difference to us."

I asked, "What difference?"

"Come with me now," she said. "Come on now, and we'll see Charlie together. I know you don't want to, but it'd mean a lot to me if you did."

I felt it was wrong that Roberta was asking something of me.

She said, in her car, "I'd like to go off now and, say, play pinball machines in some cheap bar."

As I didn't want to go to her apartment, I said, "Why don't we?"

"Do you know a place where we could play?"

"Yes."

"Where?"

"In the bar I go to, near the bus station."

Roberta laughed. The sunlight through the windscreen made all the hairs that had come loose from her braid shine. She asked, "Have you ever been in love?"

"No," I answered.

She gave me the key and asked me to go into the apartment ahead of her. As I opened the door, I saw Charlie, in an armchair in the living room, drawing on a large sketch-book flat on his knees; he looked up, his expression unlike any I had seen on his face, twisted, but when he saw me his face went blank. Roberta was behind me.

I said to him, "Roberta and I are going to go out to play pinball, and we wondered if you'd like to join us."

"Where's Jerry?" Charlie asked Roberta.

"With your parents."

He looked back at me, waiting for me to say more.

"Well, come on," I said, "let's go."

We went into downtown Boston to a little upstairs restaurant for lunch. We sat at a table by a window which gave on to a big tree. Roberta and Charlie were silent towards one another, so I did all the talking. Often, not knowing what else to talk about, I went on about what was happening in Boston. Finally, we were silent.

I said, "Have you ever wondered about the crazy relationships among the Holy Family?"

"You've brought that up before," Roberta said.

I said, "I'd like to know some reason why their relationships are held up to us as an example."

"I know," Charlie said.

Roberta said to him, "Now you're going to make one of your funny observations."

"I'll try to make it funny. I suppose we need a laugh."

"Tell me," I said to him.

"It makes sense to have over us examples of a world that makes no sense," he said, "so that we don't expect our world to make sense. And yet, however nonsensical all the relationships of the Holy Family are, we know that they have great love for one another, they up there, and they are models for us down here to love one another as greatly as they do. What we learn from them is that love has to be irrational."

Roberta said, "Don't count too much on that."

On the way back to their apartment, we stopped to pick up Jerry.

19

———•———

I knew some definite change had turned me around inside when, alone in the museum one free afternoon, I stopped before that torso of a boy on a black plinth which I had studied as a student, and I saw it as standing above the world, beyond anyone's individual and jealous attempt to possess it.

If ever I wrote a novel, I thought, it would have to be saved, if it was in any way worthy of being saved, by something occurring in it which had nothing to do with me. Anything moral in my writing would have nothing to do with me. It is absolutely true, I thought, that the greatest works of art are those created not for men but for God, whose ambition is that humankind should be one in its love for God.

As I was walking through the Fens, I heard a voice say: "Call Henry."

In a telephone booth that smelled of urine, I called his work number at the library and was told that he was at home. I was reluctant to call him there, because I might be disturbing him; but I felt generous, and it was as if I would, by calling him, show him how generous I was.

His not answering made grey feelings come back which I thought had gone.

He answered.

I said, "I hope I'm not disturbing you."

He asked me to come over.

The sunlight was horizontal, and Boston appeared to extend sideways in long, narrow shadows.

Henry answered the door in his bathrobe. He was unshaven, his hair messed, and his skin was moist.

"I've got a fever," he said.

As I followed him into his bedroom, which I had thought I would never enter again, I imagined I was returning after a long trip to a place which amazed me for existing, never mind existing unchanged. I was surprised that the same carpet was by the bed, the same lamp on the bedside table.

Then Henry did this most remarkable thing: he took off his bathrobe and stood naked for a moment before he threw it onto a chair and got into his bed. What struck me about his pale body was how devoid of sex it was. He pulled the sheet over his chest.

As I watched him, I thought that the feelings coming over me couldn't have to do with sex, though with some desire.

Sitting back to watch him more closely in a moment of silence, I felt, with a sudden outbreak of sweat, all my love for Henry come back to me as if it had never gone.

Henry was ill, but he was not going to die. My longing was for him to die, my longing was to lie down by him and hold him dead. My chest heaved for the hopelessness I felt towards such a pleasure, which was the pleasure I imagined of sitting on a fallen pillar in a destroyed city, weeping for such destruction. I must, I thought, accept that the pleasure of destruction was the only pleasure allowed me, and for that pleasure I became an altogether destructive person. The more I wanted to see Henry dead the more I felt my love for him.

His lips parched, he said, "I feel so hot."

"Shouldn't you see a doctor?" I asked.

"I'll be all right. It's just the grippe."

"Is there anything I can do?"

"I wondered if you could go out and get me some aspirin. I don't have any."

"You don't take care of yourself," I said.

On my way to the drugstore, I thought my desire to see Henry dead was a fantasy I had affected because I could only trust myself to love someone dead. I bought the aspirin, and returning up the hill thought my desire for Henry was something else, perhaps

141

worse, than to see him dead. I had not gone as far as was possible in my desire for him.

He'd given me the key and I let myself into his apartment. It was odd that Henry didn't have anyone else in his life but me who would go buy him aspirin.

In the kitchen, I filled a glass with water. I didn't want to go in to him, as if I was worried what feelings he would finally reveal to me there. For the moment, my feeling was that he had used me by sending me for the aspirin. But this feeling was just to block my anticipation of the other feelings that were waiting for me in his room. It was as if not only he, but others were waiting for me, and I couldn't imagine who they were. They had come unexpectedly.

But when I held the aspirin out to him with a glass of water and he swallowed them down with gulps, I felt a kind of pity for him. I sat in a chair by his bed.

He said, "The worst part is that I haven't been able to work."

The work he was so keen on wasn't his library job, I was sure. I didn't know what it was, and I felt I couldn't ask, but only mention it, in all seriousness, as his work. He was probably writing a book, and I wondered if he assumed I was, too, whenever he asked about my work.

He raised a hand. His voice was hoarse. "I'm not sure it matters."

"It matters."

His head raised by two pillows, he looked into the air for a moment, then at me. "What've you been up to?"

I smiled but I didn't say anything.

Then Henry, licking his lips, raised himself on his arms, perhaps to cool himself, and the damp sheets fell away from his chest and thighs, so, again, I saw his body, and I knew that my desire, which, because I must think the worst about myself, I had imagined was the desire to see the end of Henry, was not a desire at all, but a great fear. I was frightened that I would never again see Henry; it was not he who would die in himself, but would die in me. I couldn't let that happen. But, in the presence of his sick body, the fantasy was not strong enough to make him glow with health, so he fell back into his sheets and his body repelled me. If there was any desire in this fear, it was only the desire to leave.

I said, shifting in the chair, "Maybe you want to sleep."

"No," he said.

I couldn't say anything. To see him as he was now was to see, not only his body, but everything promised by his body destroyed. He was a young man not much different from me. I could not accept the revelation.

What was happening to that body, come from outside the world and standing above the world, which the world loved?

When I thought, What could he have meant to me? I got up from my chair.

He wasn't going to hold me, because, I recognized, he never tried to hold anyone against his wishes. But he said, "You just got here."

"I've got to go."

He didn't ask me why I'd called him. If he had, I wouldn't have been able to answer.

20

———————•———————

In my room, I took off my shoes and a sock. One sock on, I walked about the room hitting the edges of the furniture with the other.

I had always, I thought, prayed for a presence to appear to me – a presence so abstract it had no qualities, and all my efforts would be to give it qualities. I had always hoped to bring down spirit into matter. What I knew I couldn't do was to force spirit up from matter. I wanted to start with everything, and work to make something. It wasn't in me to start with something and make it everything, and yet this was what I must do if I was to have what I needed to live.

But everything I created embarrassed me. Against my embarrassment, I would have to contrive something, to make it stand above my embarrassment and, if nothing more, shock. At the risk of being cruel, so as not to make a joke of myself, I must try to imagine a presence which could do anything – which could be, with the darkest intentions, cruel, and never joke, and could incise with a knife the skin of a naked body, then cut deeper into the flesh and open the wounds to the bone, then, to cause the most pain, insert burning thorns into the wounds. I stopped this fantasy, but thought the only real creativity was to create pain, which couldn't be falsified. I shook my head.

I had to believe that what I wanted was not false, and, as only I could give it to myself, how could I make it not false? If what I wanted was belief, how could I have it except by bringing it out of myself?

If what I wanted was faith, I must recognize that the highest abstractions were acts of will, that the most elusive faith had to be worked for, and belief in God came from making oneself believe in God. Then I thought this wasn't true, and what was true was that the highest abstractions of thought simply occurred of themselves, that faith simply occurred, that faith in God simply occurred.

All my contradictory observations seemed uninteresting to me. What was impossible was uninteresting.

I fell on my bed.

I was taken up by a presence that came down to me and picked me up.

Images from my love making with Henry came to me, image after image, of him bright in his amazing beauty. These images came from beyond my inability to create such images. They filled me with joy.

Then I saw in his eyes when he looked at me that he wasn't making love with me, but struggling with me. He hadn't come down to make love with me. He had come to dispossess me of my continuing love for him, to dispossess me of all the images of love making. His eyes were blank. He could do it; he could remove himself entirely from me; he could do anything. But I was not going to let him do this.

Even if he had come down to save me from what we both knew was a meaningless possession, and which it should give me pleasure to see destroyed, I would not let him do it. I would turn the struggle with him into love making, and I would make our love making meaningful. Henry was trying to lift from me the stark image of himself. I restrained him. His forehead furrowed and his eyes filled with tears. He didn't want me to suffer this image. I held on to him, trying to hold his arms as they went through me, trying to kiss his face as it went into mine. I would not let go.

"Let go," he said quietly.

I turned him over and over on the bed, struggling with him.

If what I was struggling for was faith, I had not even reconciled in myself how that faith was to be achieved, through my own

145

will or a vast will-lessness. I would never reconcile these. I was struggling both to overcome and to be overcome, and in doing this I was struggling for the realization of my greatest desire, for belief.

There were meanings, there were meanings, there were. The image of Henry meant, had to mean, for the overwhelmingly simple fact of my being aware of it, more than I could say. I loved it.

How could the very person who revealed faith to me destroy it? That couldn't be. How could he, any less than I, not want everything, because only in everything could we be whole. How could he not want to go with me again as far as we'd gone, again and forever? If he gave in, we would go there, turning and turning about one another, our struggle the struggle to go further. It was only with him that I could have what I needed, and he would not take it from me.

When I forced my mind to concentrate, precisely, on his face, his arm, his thigh, I saw less and less. I saw nothing.

I retained only the sense of everything, without any particular sense, and this was embodied abstractly as nothing but a great need. I needed to have happen again what had happened, and I needed it because it was general, because only the general promised. But that sense was so general, perhaps I would not have it even if I did make love with Henry again, because it no longer had anything to do with our love making. If my senses at their most acute in making love could not give it to me, I could only imagine it existed by an act of faith. I know it did exist, because it had changed me into someone essentially different from the person I had been. That was what I could not believe would never happen again. I had to believe I could be made different, by nothing more than someone touching me or looking at me or saying a word to me. This wouldn't happen. But it would happen. I was not different. But I was different.

I imagined shouting out.

I would not let everything go. Because my love for Henry was irrelevant to the world, it was only by meaning more than the world that it had meaning at all. He meant everything to me, he had to mean everything, and my faith in the idea of such meaning was all the faith I had. Here was the moment for me to make an act of faith, an act that would realize, in a flash, what was so near. And I could make it, it was in me to make it, as it was in me to do everything. I could, I could. I could destroy. I could make. I could now, with faith, do what I had imagined was impossible. I could believe that every thought I had about another person was an expression of universal love.

A total sense of absurdity was my blessing. I would not let myself be destroyed by the absurdity. That would be my act of will; to refuse to give up everything because it is ridiculous. No. But the fact that my desire for faith should be inspired by a neurotic obsession for someone I could not have, made that desire neurotic, too. It did not refer to anything outside itself, and any attempt to make it refer to what was outside only made the desire more ridiculous, more and more ridiculous. No. The desire did have relevance outside itself, it did. It was not ridiculous. But I couldn't give relevance to it myself; someone else must do this for me. I could do it on my own; I could make it happen. I couldn't. It could only happen by being made to happen by another. It could only happen beyond my intention to have it happen. And it wouldn't happen. It would. I would make it happen. I would realize my faith by the strongest act of will. It was in me to be that strong. But then it wasn't, and something stronger than my will had to sustain the faith. No, I would have belief. I could believe, I could, but why would I not allow myself to?

I must get Henry to be aware as I was aware, I must get him to see that our true natures were more than human, that we could have everything, if we believed we could. He must love, as I loved, what we'd known in making love.

He must at least allow me the image of him I carried around with me with so much adoration that I could not sleep, or ever be really awake.

But Henry's most convincing reason for my not loving the image was that it would never perform the miracle I hopelessly expected of it, because it did not refer to anything. For an image to be real, it must reveal a need beyond ours, in which alone our need could be satisfied. It must reveal everything. I must destroy images, all, which came from me as an effort to realize my need.

Henry told me no image was going to come to me, no apparition, from beyond imagination. No images, ever, had come from afar and revealed what was beyond imagination, but came, everywhere, from the selfish imaginations of the people who had created them to realize their human desires. These images were not real because they referred only to such human desires. All images were false, and all images in the world should be destroyed.

My mind, suddenly unable to think, stopped for a moment, and Henry, wrapped in a sheet and holding something in his folded arms, left me.

He left me with a desire for faith that was impossible, one that pulled my skin, my hair, with the demand to be made possible, to be realized immediately. There was nothing I could do but ask myself where such desire came from. Where did such awareness, never to be fulfilled, come from? Why was there such a sense of promise in us, if the promise would never be kept? Why should we so want what we knew we would never get?

My mind searched for something to center on. Irrelevancies came to me, if they were irrelevancies. Maybe they were essentials. I had no more clean socks. It could be that my faith would be revealed to me by attending to my socks.

What survives the most extreme self-consciousness, I wondered? What survives the self-consciousness that makes you say of yourself, even at the highest moment of love making, "Fool, fool," for even presuming for the moment that you could rise above yourself? Does anything survive the derision of such moments? And what is the result of such derision but a hard determination to survive, at least, your self-condemnation as a fool? You think, All right, I'm a fool, and you live by some intention to live, and the intention is not to justify yourself in your own eyes or anyone else's, but simply to bear the condemnation. What adds to the depth of the condemnation is that you know you have exaggerated it, and that it is only a perversion of the self-centeredness you want to have all rights to. Your great exaggeration makes you a fool on a minor scale. So you tell yourself, All right, all right, I've got to stand myself as a minor fool. This takes more determination than if you were a major fool. And how can you not, with such intention, become an artificial person? You listen to the way you speak and, no matter how neutral you try to make your speech, eliminating what strikes you as affected, it still sounds affected, as much to others, you're sure, as to yourself. You want what is unintentional. That is why you long – in ways, passionately – for those states of mind which are undefined and cannot be intended. That sense of intention itself, that abstract and yet distinct state of mind before you contrive the intention – you like to ask yourself what it is. And the more abstract the sense is the more you are drawn to it for occurring unintentionally, as a sudden blessing. But you can't even allow yourself to pray for the blessing, which will make you an altogether different person, because you can't bless yourself. You can't make yourself a different person; you can only make yourself a more artificial person, you can only ever make yourself more of a fool. You want deliverance from yourself, you want those visitations upon yourself when you're made natural. What survives the extremest derision is the passion to be natural, to be pure. What survives is the most acute apprehension of those moments, just before you destroy them, when all your apprehension shifts, and you know it is possible to be other than what you are. You hate what you are, and at the same time you don't hate, because you know that your apprehension of another is wonderful. You will destroy it. Of course you will. You try to sustain some faith in it after it is gone, but you can't. The faith itself becomes an intention, and you know how false your intentions are. What accounts for such visitations, though? You have no idea, except that you have this idea: that they come to you, only for a moment, because you are aware, and you know that they will come to you with greater and greater force the more aware you are, aware of the ocean curving over the horizon, of mountain ranges, of cities at the mouths of rivers, of men farming the flat lands, of women in country shops, of young men wandering in woods, of young women swimming in green ponds, of people in cities walking the pavements and calling to one another across streets, of people in their houses eating, sleeping, making love on sheet-rumpled beds, of rugs, tables and chairs, cups and plates, mirrors, rolls of string, calendars, pencils, vases of flowers, of the world's soul itself from which the world's being is derived. All this happens in a moment. What survives self-consciousness, if anything survives, is the desire for those moments that can't be derided as false. It is a longing for the illuminating idea that precedes all thought, and perhaps all feeling – an idea that we know is the center of all true thinking and feeling. As a totally intentional person, your greatest intention is to keep yourself open to such ideas, to take such risks. Nothing will enter. But it will. Everything will enter.

Though it was after two o'clock in the morning, I dressed and went out. I walked conspicuously along the curb in the light of the street lamps. When I crossed over into the dark Public Garden, I stayed in the light to be seen, as though to let anyone who might be looking know that I was just out for a walk. There couldn't have been anyone else in the still garden to look at me, unless they, in the shadows of the trees, were still.

I wished I had drawn blood from Henry, just a little, then drawn blood from the same part of my body, from our arms or chests, and pressed his blood into mine.

Nothing was left, I thought, of our having made love.

Walking now across the Common, I imagined I saw people standing among a clump of trees.

A moist wind began to blow over the Common. Walking in the wind, I imagined I was in a place that had once been Boston. Natives from outside the city had killed everyone and burned the wooden buildings, so the city was reduced to fields and to dark woods shaking in the sea gusts.

I was following a path through the woods. In them, I expected to be met, to be taken where I had never been, and there I would undergo a conversion, one that would make me so different from what I was that it had to be beyond anything I could intend, anything I could imagine. Did I suddenly make an act of faith that such a conversion was possible? Did I?

Back in my room, I lay on the floor. I thought I lay for a long time, but when I looked at my watch I saw it was minutes. I thought, Well, you can't lie here forever, and I got up and undressed. In my bathroom, I washed socks in the washbasin. I rubbed a sock between my knuckles.

From my bed, I switched off the lamp on the side table. The room seemed large, and I lay as thoughtless as I was motionless. I imagined I heard someone in the room, heard a movement or a voice. A thrill spread over the surface of my skin. I looked out and listened. There was someone in the room, and, if I waited, he would come just close enough to the bed for me to see him in the dark.